PROTEC NECK

MAXIMIZE YOUR SETTLEMENT AFTER A CAR CRASH

BY JOSHUA R. BRUMLEY, JD-MBA

Protect Your Neck: Maximize Your Settlement after a Car Crash

987654321
First Edition
Printed in the United States of America.

Cover design by Stein Hansen
Interior layout by Dave Vasudevan, Pithy Wordsmithery
Copy editing by Nils Kuehn, Pithy Wordsmithery
Proofreading by Scott Morrow and Katharine Dvorak, Pithy Wordsmithery

ISBN: 979-8-9909210-0-9 (paperback)
ISBN: 979-8-9909210-2-3 (e-book)
ISBN: 979-8-9909210-1-6 (hardcover)

Joshua R. Brumley
Joshua@brumleylawfirm.com
brumleylawfirm.com

Library of Congress Control Number: 2024913234

Praise for *Protect Your Neck*

"Josh Brumley's clear, conversational style makes his 'how to' book for injured claimants the ideal resource for accident victims. The pain from accident-related injuries is compounded by the pain of dealing with insurance companies to get just compensation. Josh's book is a sound prescription to minimize both."

Bruce Lamb, JD
Professor, Highline College
Former insurance defense attorney with 30 years' experience

"Josh Brumley and I have worked together on personal injury litigation, and his ability to describe complex legal situations to clients is an inspiration for me and my practice. This book is helpful to clients and attorneys alike!"

Cole Douglas, JD
Partner, Cochran Douglas, PLLC

"In *Protect Your Neck*, attorney Joshua Brumley offers readers a comprehensive and informative guide to navigating a car accident's often confusing and overwhelming aftermath. As an experienced legal professional, Josh has seen firsthand the challenges that individuals face when trying to secure fair compensation after being involved in a car crash. Through clear and practical advice, he empowers readers to take control of their situation and maximize their settlement.

In today's world, where car accidents are unfortunately all too common, *Protect Your Neck* is a must-read for anyone who wants to be prepared for any potential legal challenges that may arise after a crash. Whether you are currently dealing with a car accident or want to be informed about future situations, this book will be an invaluable resource that you can refer back to repeatedly."

Tony Garguile, JD
Owner, Garguile Law, PLLC

"Beyond his legal acumen, Brumley's genuine compassion and dedication to serving his community permeate the pages of this book. Through compelling anecdotes and real-life case studies, he humanizes the law, illustrating the profound impact that dedicated advocacy can have on the lives of those affected by personal injury. His unwavering commitment to his clients' well-being serves as a poignant reminder of the noble purpose inherent in the practice of law."

Talwinder Singh, JD
Hothi Law Firm

"Josh Brumley's book is an essential guide for anyone dealing with the aftermath of a car accident. It expertly blends practical advice with real-life scenarios, offering readers crucial insights into managing injuries and navigating legal claims. This book is a must-read for those looking to understand and maximize their rights and settlements after an accident."

Allan Njoroge
Founder and CEO, Actriv Healthcare

"*Protect Your Neck* is a game changer for anyone navigating the aftermath of a car crash. What sets this book apart is Josh's unwavering commitment to his clients' well-being, evident in every page. In a world where accidents can leave us feeling helpless, this book is a beacon of hope, offering practical advice and a road map to recovery. Every person, whether they've been in a crash or not, should have access to this book!"

Camden Minervino, JD
Minervino Law

"Josh gives specific, direct advice for what to do in case you are injured—obvious, common-sense, and needed advice. You need it when you are hurt, yet these may be the last things you think of in the moment. Be a friend: share this book with others when you hear of their incidences; remind others of this collection of common-sense actions to take. This book will prepare you to work with Josh and his team at Brumley Law."

Maralise Hood Quan, JD
Executive director, Center for Dialog & Resolution

"Josh's book meets injured people where they are, which is usually a place of confusion and trauma, and guides them toward a place of confidence and resolve. I recommend it to anyone who is looking for a lifeline to legal recovery from injury after a car wreck."

John Hardie
Palace Law

"In 2021, I was involved in a car accident. As a recent arrival to the country with limited English proficiency, I found navigating the process quite challenging. Thankfully, I turned to Josh, who expertly managed my case. This book, *Protect Your Neck*, details all the dilemmas I faced and presents them in a clear and accessible manner. Josh effectively explains how traffic accidents are handled, making the information easy to understand."

Ali Al-Azzawi, م. عـلاء العــزاوي
Accident reconstruction artist

"In the unfortunate situation of a motor-vehicle collision, Josh's book offers a resource that can help inform and enable readers to know their rights while seamlessly navigating the intricacies of a personal injury claim."

Rai Nauman Mumtaz, MPH, MPA
MD student
President, Center for Dialog & Resolution Board of Directors
Member, Tyee Sports Council, Washington Athletics

"As someone deeply immersed in the field of liability research, I can recognize an authentic and dedicated personal injury attorney when I see one. Josh Brumley's *Protect Your Neck* stands out as a beacon of practical and invaluable advice for anyone navigating the often-confusing landscape of personal injury law. His expertise shines through on every page, making complex legal concepts accessible to the everyday individual. This book is a must-read for those seeking clear, actionable guidance in protecting their rights and securing the justice they deserve."

Grady Escobar
Founder of Coastal Research

"Having a notable guide on the 'how' and 'why' of prioritizing your needs in an adverse situation is vital. The duality of Joshua's expertise and empathy in these measures clearly shows that there are those willing to help and go the extra mile in ensuring your protection and well-being. Know that he and his team have your back in your time of need."

Marisela Sampaga-Smith

Dedicated to my dear friend Jordan, who passed away in 2023 due to complications from a motor-vehicle accident.

Table of Contents

Preface

I was 21 years old and driving back to college along a relatively busy road after having lunch in Tacoma. My day was going great until, out of nowhere, a car pulled out of a parking lot right in front of me. Although I was driving at the posted speed limit of 35 MPH, there was no way I could slow down in time to avoid an accident. I ended up T-boning the other car, totaling both vehicles. Airbags deployed. Immediately afterward, I found myself not having a clue as to what I should do in that moment.

Nothing prepares you for being in an impact like that.

I hit the other car with such force that, for a few seconds, I thought I might die. If I hadn't been wearing my seatbelt, I probably would have. Both cars were destroyed. Looking back, the whole incident is a blur. I was in pain—and in shock. I didn't know what to do. Did I need an ambulance? Or the police? Should I have immediately checked on the other driver? I wondered whether they would try to say that the accident was my fault. How would I get around without a car? Did I have any broken bones? There was a shooting pain in my neck, and I was scared to move.

That accident changed my life. A number of my injuries caused long-term chronic pain that I am still working on managing to this day. But thankfully, those injuries weren't the primary way my life altered course after the accident. Being in that situation opened my eyes to the unique challenges of being injured in a car accident that wasn't my fault. Nothing had prepared me for it—and I was suddenly thrust into a world I didn't understand, where virtually everything was on the line. I hired an attorney, but he wasn't much help in terms of explaining the situation and next steps. It was hard to get a hold of him whenever I had a question, so I eventually decided to just stop asking and make peace with the fact that I would continue to have no idea what was going on. I wondered if that's just how things are for car-accident victims.

The physical pain was practically consuming me, and I didn't know where to start when it came to finding the right doctors to treat my injuries. On top of all that, I still had to go about my regular life—showing up for work and passing my college classes. It was, without a doubt, the most stressful time of my life.

I'm still dealing with injuries that I've never been fully compensated for. Yet if I could go back and change what happened, I actually wouldn't. That's because if it weren't for that accident and its aftermath, I never would have discovered my passion for being a personal injury attorney. I'm able to understand how my clients feel because I have been in their shoes. I know what it's like to feel confused and vulnerable. And so I help my clients in the ways that I wish I would have been helped by my attorney.

Over the years, I've represented countless clients, recovering millions of dollars in settlements. I founded a highly successful personal injury firm in Washington state, and I've been expanding our offices to serve more people. I believe our success is due in large part to my MBA and my experience as a college law professor and being able to translate complex legal issues into bite-sized, manageable chunks of information. I use these same skills as a board member for the Center for Dialog & Resolution, a non-profit mediation center in Tacoma that helps to peacefully resolve high-conflict legal situations.

I wish that no one had a need for my services. But until every car is self-driving and 100-percent safe—or we figure out how to teleport—there will always be car accidents and people who are injured in them.

If you or a loved one has been injured in a car accident, I hope this book helps you to feel more equipped to go through this process—with or without me as your attorney. Follow the chapters in this book closely and know that things will get better. I'm with you every step of the way.

Introduction

The average American spends 60.2 minutes in the car each day, covering an average of 30.1 miles.[1] With all that time behind the wheel, it's easy to see how there are upwards of 20,000 car crashes in the United States every day. That's 14 each minute.[2] When you think about such factors as distracted driving, poor weather conditions, and simple human error, we're all vulnerable.

No matter how common car accidents are, you're never ready when it happens to you; they usually come out of nowhere when you least expect it. In the blink of an eye, it can change your life forever. When a collision wasn't your fault, the aftermath can be especially overwhelming, leaving you grappling with physical injuries, emotional distress, and a labyrinth of legal complexities.

> *In the blink of an eye, it can change your life forever.*

I often get calls from new clients who are still at the scene of their accident. Many are in a state of shock or disbelief. Their minds are foggy, and they struggle to explain what happened. Others are furious. Adrenaline is pumping through their veins, and they scream into the phone about what an idiot the other driver is. Others call me crying, in pain and terrified. They worry about the extent of their injuries, along with the well-being of both their passengers and the people involved. They're concerned about the accident becoming a catalyst that sparks financial instability. How will they get to work if they are injured and don't have transportation? Will their insurance go up and become unaffordable? For many people, just the thought of having to interact with the police is enough to induce serious anxiety. From there, insurance companies and attorneys will need to be brought in, and that adds to the stress level because people don't know what will happen next or what will be expected of them. Will they end up having to sue a good person who made just a simple driving mistake? Or will they get scammed by the other party if that person denies that they were at fault? People picture themselves getting into an ugly situation and having to testify in court. Those who don't have citizenship wonder whether the accident will cause problems with immigration.

What could be more stressful and anxiety-inducing than all this? The answer is not much! Being in a major car accident can be one of the worst events in a person's life. But let me tell you the most important thing to know: **after the dust settles, things can either get better or get worse depending on how the situation is handled.**

The aftermath of being in a car accident can go in one of two totally different directions because the at-fault driver—or, more accurately, their insurance company—has a lot to lose. Depending on the severity of the accident, this could be thousands, hundreds of thousands, or even millions of dollars. If they can minimize this expense, they certainly will. Insurance is a for-profit industry—and those companies don't give money away out of the goodness of their hearts. Although there are plenty of good people who work for insurance companies, their job is to minimize their cost of doing business. And they're good at it. Many are great, actually. They're experts who handle this kind of thing day in and day out.

And you're just an average person who doesn't know what to expect. Imagine you're playing chess against a grand master and you only just learned the rules of the game yesterday from Google. That's not a fair fight.

Depending on the actions you take in the days and months following your accident, you could walk away with enough to cover your medical bills, as well as compensation for pain and suffering. Or you could walk away with nothing. You only get one shot at this, and you need to make it count.

In *Protect Your Neck*, I provide a road map for every step of the journey—from what to do at the scene of the accident through the long-term recovery process. You'll discover crucial insights for protecting your rights, seeking the care you need, and keeping more money in your pocket. It's like having access to an attorney 24/7 to answer questions you didn't even know you should be asking.

The chapters are written so that they make sense in chronological order from right after the time an accident occurs. If you've been in an accident and a lot of time has passed, feel free to skip to the chapters that are most relevant to you at this time, but know that you will still have valuable knowledge to gain from reading the book in its entirety.

Here's a sneak preview of what to expect:

Chapter 1: What to Do Immediately after a Crash. Learn the most important things you can do to show you were not at fault so that you can protect the value of your case. From documenting the accident with photos to understanding the police report and not talking to insurance companies, this chapter has you covered.

Chapter 2: Personal Injury 101. When you've been injured in a car accident, there's a good chance you're totally unfamiliar with the legal process for personal injury cases. This chapter explains the basics and gives a summary of key milestones and timelines.

Chapter 3: Working with an Attorney. If you don't have a background in law, choosing the right attorney/law firm can be difficult. How can you tell if you have solid representation you can trust? And how much will a good attorney cost you? This chapter gives you an insider's look at everything you need to know.

Chapter 4: Understanding Insurance Coverage. Though most of us have auto insurance, only a select few fully understand what it covers. Insurance might not be the most exciting topic, but policy details can mean the difference in taking home a settlement you deserve or nothing at all. This chapter helps you understand what your case could be worth, and it might change how you think about buying insurance moving forward.

Chapter 5: What to Know When You're Injured. When you've been injured in a car accident, there is a liability component that puts you in a different situation than being injured in other ways. A settlement could cover your medical expenses and compensate you for pain and suffering, but getting what you deserve will take time and effort. Learn the key considerations and find out how to mitigate any further risks.

Chapter 6: Types of Injuries and Treatment. Certain injuries are extremely common in car accidents. By recognizing symptoms early on, you can prevent complications for your health—and your case—down the road. From whiplash to soft-tissue injuries, we explore the signs and symptoms that indicate that you are in need of medical attention, as well as the types of treatment that are available.

Chapter 7: General Damages and Pain and Suffering. There are many ways a person can be negatively impacted by an accident. From physical pain to loss of enjoyment in life, a serious injury can create a butterfly effect that ripples through your life. Your new normal can be quite different from your old one. It's essential to make sure that all these negative impacts are carefully considered when resolving your case.

Chapter 8: Special Damages. Getting into an accident can be a hard hit to your wallet. From an ER visit to fixing your car to the paychecks you miss because you're laid up at home, the cost of being injured adds up quickly. In this chapter, we discuss what should be considered part of the value of your case.

Chapter 9: Paths to Resolution—Settling Your Case. Ninety percent of personal injury cases are settled out of court. In this chapter, I demystify the negotiation process between your attorney and the insurance adjuster or defense attorney. You'll learn the myriad reasons your case is likely to settle—whether it happens quickly or right before your trial date.

Chapter 10: The Litigation Process. Once a lawsuit is filed, there is a specific process that both sides follow. In this chapter, I give you a breakdown of what to expect during these milestones, including the discovery process, depositions, and appearing in court. You'll learn the most important things to know about going in front of a judge or jury and how to put your best foot forward.

Chapter 11: Getting Paid and Moving On. As you reach the final step in your journey, there are a few important things you'll need to keep in mind. From being smart with your money to reducing your chances of being in a situation like this again in the future, this chapter provides some closing comments you won't want to miss.

When you've been injured in a car accident, there's a lot to know about moving forward, but *Protect Your Neck* has you covered. It's more than just a guide; it's a lifeline when you find yourself at the intersection of vulnerability and injustice. Keep reading to arm yourself with the knowledge you need to regain control of your physical health, finances, and emotional well-being during this trying time.

CHAPTER 1

What to Do Immediately after a Crash

As a personal injury attorney, I've come to learn that your health is the most important thing. Health is wealth! After you've been injured, not only do you have to endure physical pain, but your quality of life is also compromised. And my job is to fight for you. I want you to be in the best position possible to be made whole after being in an accident. At the bare minimum, this will require compensation for you to pay your medical bills. It's also possible that you could be awarded a sum of money for pain, suffering, and the impact on the quality of your life.

But there's one crucial caveat for helping you win your case and getting you the settlement money you deserve: *we have to be able to prove that the accident was not your fault.* If we can't do that, or at least make a strong argument that could win over a jury, the other side (meaning the other person's insurance company) is unlikely to voluntarily accept liability. The reason behind this is simple: if the driver they represent was at fault, it costs them money. Depending on the severity of the accident, we could be talking about tens of thousands, hundreds of thousands, or even millions of dollars per case. Insurance companies are for-profit businesses, and their goal is to keep as much money in their pocket as possible. It might seem callous, but your accident is just a cost of doing business. They will try to minimize that cost every single time.

The most effective way to do that is to deny that the driver they represent was at fault.

Determining fault for an accident can be tricky in certain situations because it's not always black and white; fault can be argued and interpreted in different ways. For example, if a crash happens because someone messes up big time and you mess up a little, it's possible that 1 to 50 percent of the fault is yours. Determining what's fair in that situation will take effort from you and your attorney—and there is a lot on the line. That's why it's so important to take certain steps at the scene of an accident and in the following couple days to support your case as much as possible and protect yourself from being taken advantage of.

Let's be clear about your situation: accidents often come down to your word against another's. I've seen plenty of cases where a driver knew that they'd caused an accident and then blatantly lied about it to police and their insurance company. They say that the other driver was the one who was speeding or ran a red light. People do this all the time because they are afraid of what will happen to them if they tell the truth. They're scared that their insurance premiums will go up, they'll get an expensive ticket, or they might even lose their driver's license. They may be deeply embarrassed that they'd made such a costly mistake, and it's difficult for them to own up to it. So instead of telling the truth, they either completely deny responsibility or they try to share it with the victim (e.g., "I wouldn't have hit them if they weren't speeding.").

When a driver says that they weren't at fault, their insurance company is much more likely to back them up and also refuse to accept liability. That's why it's important that you collect evidence that will support you.

The very first thing you should do is to take a photo of the other vehicle's license plate. That way, if at any point they try to skirt responsibility and leave the scene of the accident, you have evidence and aren't left high and dry. From there, you need to get strategic.

Safety First

When you've been injured in a car crash, you are in a vulnerable situation. Your car might be in the middle of the freeway in the path of oncoming traffic or upside down in the middle of nowhere. You don't know who's in the other car. They might be a sweet old lady or an irate criminal with a gun. The last thing you need is to put yourself at more risk. Be conservative and prioritize your physical safety. Determine whether it's safer for you to stay in your car or get out. If the other driver starts being aggressive with you, don't engage. Wait for first responders to arrive.

Document What Happened

Always call 911. Even if the accident seems minor, you want to get police and, if need be, EMS involved right away. Getting an accurate police report is the best way to document the accident and protect yourself from the other side saying *you* were at fault.

Let's address the fact that some people are uncomfortable dealing with police. They don't trust law enforcement and they try to avoid them at all costs. The other driver might be in this camp, and they could try to convince you not to call the cops. It's good to be aware that some people have even greater motivation not to call the police. They could be driving on a suspended license or without insurance, or even have a warrant out for their arrest. Or maybe they have illegal drugs in their car, or they're intoxicated. If you're being pressured not to call 911 and get police involved, do not give in. If you are injured in a car wreck and were not at fault, you don't have anything to gain from not calling 911. In fact, it puts you at a huge disadvantage. The other driver could report the accident later and say that you were at fault and drove away, which would create a major problem for your case.

Even if you were the one who was driving without a license or insurance, that has nothing to do with whether you were at fault in an accident. Yes, you might get a ticket, but that's a small price to pay to get the medical treatment you need and receive thousands of dollars in settlement money.

Bottom line: do not be afraid to call the police. It's generally much better for you if they are able to come to the scene of the accident and document it in a police report. As a neutral third party, their assessment of the accident carries more weight than what either driver says.

While you're waiting for the police and perhaps EMS to arrive, it's up to you whether you want to speak with the other driver. Sometimes it can be smart to do this because people are more likely to be honest in the moment before they've had time to think about what they should say to protect themselves. They have less of a filter, which works in your favor.

Several years ago, I was in an accident in which I was rear-ended by another vehicle. When I asked the driver what happened, he admitted, "Sorry, I wasn't even looking at my phone. I was looking at all that wood back there." (We had just passed a lumber yard where there was, in fact, quite a lot of wood.)

Once a person admits that they were at fault, they are much less likely to go back on it later. When the police arrived on the scene, I told them what the guy had told me, they asked him about it, and he verified that's what happened. The officer then noted in his report that the other driver was indeed at fault.

This is the best-case scenario for liability: the driver readily admits fault at the scene, and that gets documented in the police report. This is what you should go for when talking with the other driver. Unfortunately, most of the time, it's not that easy.

When the police arrive at the scene, you will want to communicate as much information as you can to show that the other driver was at fault. Be honest and explain what happened. If you have reason to believe they are intoxicated, say so. Be careful not to overshare about yourself, as there's always a risk you might say something that could be misinterpreted and used against you.

The officer will talk to the other driver as well, assess the scene, and fill out a police report. The report should include important information about the accident, such as the following:

- Date, time, and location
- Weather and road conditions
- Description and identification of each vehicle involved, including make, model, color, and license-plate number
- Insurance information for each vehicle
- Names, addresses, phone numbers, and driver's-license information for all drivers involved
- Information about passengers, if applicable
- A description or diagram detailing how the accident occurred and illustrating the positions of vehicles before, during, and after the collision
- Names, addresses, phone numbers, and statements from any witnesses
- Description of injuries sustained by individuals involved in the accident
- Assessment of damage to vehicles and other property
- Any traffic violations or citations issued at the scene
- Any of the police officer's own observations

As you can see, this is a lot of information, and in a perfect world, police reports would always be 100-percent complete and accurate. Unfortunately, that is not reality. Police officers are frequently in a hurry, and they don't record all the information that you would ideally need to support your case. Sometimes reports include errors such as misspelled names, incorrect license-plate numbers, or the omission that there were passengers in the vehicles.

In some cases, you might not even be able to get a police officer to come out to the scene of your accident because they are dealing with more important issues. You might be asked to file the report yourself online or drive down to a local station to complete it there.

Regardless of whether a police officer arrives at the scene of your accident, you should do your best to document what happened and collect your own evidence. Tell the other driver you'd like to take a photo of their driver's license and insurance documents. Also take plenty of photos of the accident, including the vehicle damage and where the cars lay after the impact. This evidence can be the difference in winning your case, and you will be the only person at the scene who is concerned about this. Don't expect the cops to care enough about liability to take any photos at all. Their priority is getting the vehicles off the road and out of the way of traffic. Once the cars are moved, liability evidence is lost, so it's important to take photos right away. You should also document any relevant road signs or signals. Look around to see if you spot any cameras that might have caught the accident on video. (Sometimes a Ring camera at someone's front door will capture the scene of an accident.) If the accident involved a bike or motorcycle, be sure to take extra notes and photos of any crosswalks, bike lanes, sidewalks, and intersections that may be relevant—and also skid marks, which can be used to measure speed. Nuances and details matter.

I realize that this can be a lot to ask from you, particularly if you've just been injured in a car crash. You would be in pain and probably also in fight, flight, or freeze mode. If you're unable to get out of your car to take photos and record the information that should be in the police report, that's OK. Ask a witness or bystander to help you or call a friend who's close enough to the scene to get there quickly. It might seem like a lot to deal with at the time, but it's critical for setting your case up for success.

Seek Medical Care

Once you establish who was at fault in your accident, the focus of your case becomes the severity of your injuries. Downplaying the medical consequences is a key strategy insurance companies employ to minimize their cost of doing business. After all, if you aren't that injured, they shouldn't have to pay that much money to make you whole, right?

Calling 911 right after the impact will ensure you get immediate medical attention if you need it. (As stated earlier, you want the police to come out anyway, so you always want to call 911, even if your injuries are minor.) If you don't need an ambulance, you should start making plans to see a licensed doctor ASAP—definitely within 48 hours. I cannot stress this enough: time is of the essence. You can go to the ER, urgent care, or see a primary-care provider.

Let's be honest: there are some people who don't like going to the doctor. They tough it out unless they're practically dying, and then and only then will they seek care. Reluctance, or avoidance, of the healthcare system can be due to many reasons, but when it comes to car accidents, you need to get over it. Immediately. Here's why:

- **It's harder to prove that you were injured if you don't seek treatment immediately.** Insurance companies are looking for reasons to show that injuries did not result from an accident. If you don't see a doctor right after an accident, it becomes much easier to argue that you were never injured in the first place or that your injuries were so minor that you didn't need medical care. And if you didn't need care then, why would you need it now? If you have a serious injury that you didn't seek care for until several days or weeks later, insurance companies can argue that you were injured some other way and are trying to blame it on this accident in order to get settlement money. You don't want to go down the road of making it harder to prove that you were injured.

- **Injuries are often more serious than they seem immediately after a car crash.** When you've been in an accident, your adrenaline is likely to be so high that you can't feel pain like you normally would. In fact, this can go on all day. When you wake up the next morning, you're likely to feel drained, emotionally exhausted, and physically tense. It's easy to think that you'll feel better in a couple days after you get some rest, but when that time passes, maybe you'll realize you can't twist your neck to look over your shoulder. Or there's a new kind of pain in your back, along with some numbness, tingling, or mobility issues. This can end up being much more severe than you realize. The human body is complex, and there's a good chance you need medical tests (e.g., an X-ray or MRI) to fully understand the extent of your injuries.

- **You aren't saving money by forgoing medical treatment.** Whether it's health insurance, doctor's bills, or prescriptions, healthcare expenses in the United States can be crazy expensive. If you're injured, you might think you can't afford treatment or that it would be better to go without treatment if you can. This is a bad decision and can cause the opposite effect of what you're intending. If you try to minimize your care and rehabilitation costs, what you're actually doing is minimizing the settlement money you're likely to get later. If you're truly in pain, do not forgo treatment, especially in the initial weeks after your accident.

The lesson here is to make sure you seek immediate care from a licensed medical professional. If you want to explore other types of treatment as well, such as massage or acupuncture, that's totally fine, but insurance companies will not recognize such treatments the same way they would as you seeing a licensed doctor.

Next Steps to Protect Yourself

After calling 911, your next call should be to an attorney. It's important to get good legal representation—now. Ideally, your attorney would start working on your case as soon as possible. There are things they can do the day of the accident, and in the following days, that will make your life immediately easier.

One key responsibility of your attorney is to protect you from the other driver's insurance company. Whenever an accident happens, each party's insurance company is notified. The individuals working on the case will mainly be adjusters or claims representatives. It's their job to try to settle a case quickly, either by refusing to accept that their driver was at fault (and thus paying nothing to the other person) or by offering as small a settlement as possible to the other person to get them to go away.

Adjusters will easily obtain your phone number, and you will definitely be getting a call from them within a day or two after the accident. However, you are not obligated to speak to them, and nothing good would come from the call. Unfortunately, adjusters are very skilled at making it seem like they are the good guys. Whenever they call an accident victim, it typically goes something like this:

"I heard you were in a car accident yesterday. Are you OK? ... Wow, that sounds scary ... I'm so glad you're feeling better today. I was worried about you. Listen, I know how hard it can be to have your car in the shop. I'm able to offer you $1,000 today. That should cover the damage on your car and give you some leftover cash to get a few massages. You deserve it after everything you've been though. If that sounds good, I'll mail you a check this afternoon to make sure you get taken care of right away."

Adjusters always sound so friendly. They ask questions that make it seem like they care about you and want to help. Do not be fooled. The call is always recorded and they make a living from using your words against you.

Think about it: if a for-profit company is going to call you out of the blue and offer you a sizeable check (almost always $500, $1,000, or $1,500), it's unlikely they are doing it from the goodness of their hearts. Instead, it's a sign that they know that the driver they represent was at fault. If you are injured in an accident and the other driver was at fault, their insurance company owes you money. Whatever they are offering you up front with no questions asked is far less than what you deserve.

But unless you've been in this situation before, how would you know that you're being taken advantage of? After all, a thousand dollars might sound like a lot of money, and getting a check in a couple of days can feel like instant gratification.

The problem is that you don't know what your case is worth. In fact, no one knows exactly what your case is worth yet because there hasn't been enough time to accurately assess injuries or pain and suffering. That's another key reason you shouldn't blindly accept a settlement.

You might be wondering if it's OK to talk to your own insurance company. Beware of one potential downfall of doing so without having an attorney in your corner: you and the other party could have the same insurance company. You wouldn't know that you might be speaking against your self-interest. (This is another reason why it's a good idea to get the other driver's insurance information at the scene of the accident.)

Sometimes I get calls from people who were injured in an accident months or even years ago. They'd accepted the adjuster's initial offer without consulting an attorney but didn't realize the extent of their injuries. They then ended up spending thousands in medical bills and were still in pain. They ask if we can go back and get proper compensation for what they've been through. I hate those calls because I feel so bad for the people. Once they sign the insurance company's release and cash the check, it's over. There's nothing anyone can do to go back and get more money. Victims get taken advantage of by insurance companies all the time. They accept $500 when they should have gotten $50,000. This is why you should never talk to the other party's insurance company—even if they keep calling you and offering you slightly more money.

Once you sign on with an attorney, they will make sure the other driver's insurance company is no longer allowed to contact you directly. All communications go through your attorney, who is able to assess the quality of the offers and negotiate on your behalf.

In the next chapter, I'll go over a breakdown of the basic steps you can expect to take in your case. Although every case is different, it's helpful to know the general processes and timelines for personal injury cases.

Key Takeaways

- Document the scene of the accident. Take plenty of photos.
- Call 911.
- Get a police report. (File your own report if needed.)
- Check the report for accuracy.
- Make sure you're seen by an urgent-care doctor or your primary-care doctor within 48 hours.
- Get an attorney.
- Don't talk to the other driver's insurance company without your lawyer (or your own insurance company if you and the other driver share the same insurance company).

CHAPTER 2

Personal Injury 101

Have you ever thought about what it might be like to appear in court? It's easy to recall TV shows and movies of high-pressure trials where someone is sweating it out on the witness stand while an attorney dials up the pressure. A judge and jury watch patiently, waiting for some kind of awful truth to be exposed. Someone might even be screaming, "The truth? You can't handle the truth!"

I can almost guarantee that your personal injury case won't look anything like that! Why? It's just not how the vast majority of these kinds of cases go. In fact, 90 percent don't even go to trial. That means both parties agree to a deal out of court, and the opposing sides most likely don't even see each other in person. As the victim of the accident, it can be very anticlimactic—which is probably a good thing because you've had more than enough drama to last you a while anyway.

Law is a notoriously complex topic. Unless your educational background is in the legal system, chances are that you have no idea what to expect when it comes to a personal injury case. And why would you? Most people hope they never have a reason to learn all about this area of the law.

The good news is that by hiring a high-quality law firm, you are able to drastically cut back on what you need to know about your case because you have experts in your corner who will be guiding you every step of the way.

But even when you have the best legal representation available, it helps to start with a basic understanding of the process, the players, and what you can expect in terms of payout. In this chapter, I cover a broad overview of what a personal injury case can look like. Consider this the 101 class. Then, after giving you a solid lay of the land, subsequent chapters go into greater detail about what to expect in the various stages of your journey.

Getting Paid

Most car-accident victims are looking for the light at the end of the tunnel; they want to receive just compensation. After all, that's the whole point of going down this legal path! Let's start here so that we're on the same page with where compensation can come from. When you're injured in a car crash, you can recover money from a couple different sources:

- **The other party's insurance company (a.k.a. "third party"):** In most cases where car-accident victims recover money, it comes from the at-fault driver's insurance company.

- **Your insurance company (a.k.a. "first party"):** In some situations, the car-accident victim's insurance company will provide compensation. This can happen if the victim was hit by an uninsured or underinsured motorist (which, for example, is nearly one in five cars on the road in Washington state) and the accident victim has uninsured-motorist (UIM) protection.

The total amount of money you're able to receive is completely dependent on these insurance policies. Money doesn't come from the state, the Fed, or any other organization. You

The total amount of money you're able to receive is completely dependent on these insurance policies.

shouldn't expect to receive money directly from the other driver either. Though it is possible to personally sue the other driver, it usually doesn't make sense to do so. (Most people who are driving around without insurance and causing accidents aren't exactly pillars of responsibility in other areas of their life, and they aren't usually sitting on valuable assets you could recover as compensation.)

Insurance companies and individual policies offer drastically different levels of coverage. The other driver's policy could have a maximum payout of anywhere from $25,000 to $2,000,000. That could be all that's on the table, or you might be able to supplement that amount with your own policies.

From the very beginning of the case, your attorney should have an idea of the potential payout, given the insurance policies and the severity of your accident. This will help shape your case.

What Are You Being Compensated For?

Any money you're awarded for your case is meant to cover two different forms of loss/harm:

- **Special damages.** These are specific financial repercussions you incurred because of the accident, such as hospital bills, property damage, and lost wages from the time you were unable to work. These damages have actual costs associated with them, and you can easily identify their value.
- **General damages.** This category addresses other negative impacts from an accident that don't have a set monetary value, such as pain and suffering, impact on the quality of your life, disfigurement, and inconvenience. Tying a fair monetary value to these abstract damages will be up to your attorney.

A Brief Summary of the Legal Process

Every case is different. Its timeline, the exact steps you need to take, and your strategy can vary greatly depending on a variety of factors. Some cases settle in a couple of months with very little opposition or conflict, whereas others can take more than a year to resolve. I go into some of those nuances later in the book, but for now, this is a solid breakdown of the legal process for personal injury cases.

Step 1: Do an intake and hire an attorney on a contingency fee

When you're injured in a car crash, it's up to you whether you want to hire an attorney or represent yourself. Attorneys in this practice area do not charge up front for their services and instead charge a contingency fee wherein they get paid at the end of the case only when you get paid. It is my humble opinion that every plaintiff should have representation. To help you make this decision, it's smart to reference statistics. The average settlement recovery without an attorney is $17,600, and the average settlement recovery with an attorney is $77,600. That is more than a 440-percent increase.[3] I dig into these numbers a little deeper later in the book, but the key thing to know right now is that you will almost certainly get a significantly higher settlement if you choose to have an attorney represent you.

Receiving more money from your accident is a major benefit of working with an attorney, but that certainly isn't the only reason to secure legal representation. An attorney's job is to be the liaison between you and the other players involved (e.g., insurance companies, the court system, and healthcare providers) in both the legal and post-accident recovery processes. Your attorney understands each player's role in your case, how to manage the relationships and tasks, and what to do when. They demystify the process and make everything easier for you.

Without an attorney, you will need to take the journey described in this chapter on your own. Trust me: that is not an easy task. To do it well, you will need to dedicate a massive number of hours of work and research time. If you choose to represent yourself, make sure you are able to dedicate the time and space you'll need to be effective.

6 Stages of Your

BRUMLEY LAW FIRM

Treatment

Multiple modalities of treatment are key for quick results and maximizing value. Seeing a chiropractor, physical therapist, and more is important. This is the longest stage of your case, and we can't rush. If you have questions of where to go, we can help! You will get **monthly** care calls from your case manager asking for updates and giving you tips.

Intake

In the intake stage, we a sign fee agreement and medical releases and then open your claims with the at-fault insurance company on your behalf. We also gather evidence and photos plus your health and auto insurance info.

02

03

Demand

Here we gather your medical records, bills, and costs of your case and compose a work-of-art **demand letter**. This begins the negotiation phase, and insurance companies need approximately 30 days to review and make an offer.

01

START

You also need to file an insurance claim. Your attorney will take care of this within a couple of days of hiring them. As I discuss in Chapter 1, you should not speak with the other driver's insurance company or your own insurance company without your attorney. In general, as a car-accident victim, it's better not to be involved in this process and let someone else handle it for you.

Step 2: Seek proper medical treatment

The most important thing for you to do after being injured in an accident is to focus on your recovery. I recommend seeing a variety of medical providers as part of that journey, as most of my clients

Car Accident Case

04
Negotiation

Negotiations flow back and forth between us and the insurance company, who will try to minimize the value of your claim. We don't settle your claim without your authority.

04 B
Negotiation Breakdown

Negotiations sometimes don't work out and we are forced to file a lawsuit to get the full value of your claim. A detour worth the extra time!

Closing Interview

You will be scheduled to come into the office to **receive your check** and take a photo with the team! You will also get some free swag for being a valued client of our firm.

06

Settlement

If you approve the offer from the insurance company, we begin working on finalizing the amount of outstanding bills to providers. Once we have a final settlement memo for you to sign, we will schedule your closing interview.

05

BRUMLEY LAW FIRM

do. This typically includes a primary-care provider (PCP) or family doctor and a variety of other specialists recommended by your PCP. The goal is to gain a full understanding of your injuries and what it will take to make you whole. Depending on the extent of your injuries, this can be a long process—months or perhaps even more than a year. Patience is key. You don't want to settle your case quickly only to then find out that your injuries are more severe than you initially believed. If that happens, you could miss out on the full compensation you deserve.

As you undergo treatment, you will be asked to document your recovery progress and check in regularly with the case manager at your attorney's law firm. You will need to keep all bills and records of treatment to share with them so that they can stay up to date on where you are in the recovery process. This information is needed to help them understand how much your case is worth. They should be able to give you information on your case at regular points throughout this process to make sure you are well informed.

One caveat here: sometimes medical bills easily surpass the maximum insurance payout that is available per the insurance policy. When this happens, your case can close before you're done with treatment because the insurance company willingly pays out the maximum amount.

Step 3: Prepare demand

After you've completed your medical treatment plan and you're back to 100 percent (or as close as you are able to get), your attorney will compile all your information and create a demand package that details your injuries, damages, and how much money you should be paid.

Since the details around cases can vary so much for a myriad of reasons, it's hard to know what your case could truly be worth without getting personalized insight from an attorney. That said, it might be helpful to see the national average payout for car accidents based on a few different levels of severity:

- Accident with fatalities: $1,410,000 per death
- Accident with non-fatal disabling injuries: $78,900
- Accident with non-disabling injuries and property damage: $8,900[4]

These numbers vary greatly from state to state, and in my experience in Washington specifically, these numbers are low. There is also a lot of variation depending on the nature and severity of your injuries outside the three categories listed above. Your attorney will consider these averages and how your case compares and come up with a negotiation strategy. If you agree with their plan, they will then share it with the other side.

Step 4: Negotiate

There are multiple paths to resolution, and your attorney will guide the way. After submitting the demand package, the other side could agree right away and your case would be settled ASAP. However, it's more common that your attorney will need to negotiate back and forth with the other side. This can typically take weeks or months.

If negotiations break down and it appears that the other side is not willing to offer a reasonable settlement, your attorney will file a lawsuit on your behalf. From there, you will enter mediation, which is a required legal step, as our court system simply does not have the bandwidth to address all cases, so people are encouraged to reach their own settlement deals without a judge or jury.

If mediation fails to reach a settlement, the case will then either be scheduled to go to trial (if it's worth more than $100,000) or arbitration. Notice how I said it will *be scheduled to* go to trial. That's because even when a lawsuit has been filed and the case has been given a trial date, it can settle at any time before then—and 90 percent of the time, it will. You might have to go through some of the steps to prepare for trial, such as sharing information with the other side and being available for an interview (i.e., a deposition). But chances are that at some point during the year-long lead-up to your trial date, the case will settle.

Step 5: Settle your case

After the case is over, you finally get to collect your settlement check! The insurance company typically writes the check to your law firm, which helps distribute payments to any of the parties that have outstanding bills, such as medical providers.

As a general rule, you can expect about a third of the total sum to go toward healthcare expenses, a third to go to attorneys, and the remaining third to go to you. (This is a good way to estimate roughly how much your case is worth: take your total medical expenses and multiply that number by three.) Also be aware that you won't be taxed on the money you're awarded.

After all your expenses have been paid, you should have money left over to spend however you like, and you can move on to the next phase of your life.

It's important to note that once a case is closed, it cannot be reopened, even if other evidence comes to light later or your injuries end up being more severe than you first realized.

Step 6: Conduct a closing interview

A closing interview is the process where Brumley Law Firm pays the client their portion of the settlement. This is done in person, in office, unless otherwise arranged. Other firms might call it something else or might just mail you a check.

There is a lot more to know—with plenty of nuances—about all these steps, but this is the basic overview of what you can expect. I know it can feel overwhelming to think about the coming weeks and months, so my best advice is to take it day by day and make sure you take care of yourself. This is your time to focus on your physical and mental health as you continue to recover from your accident.

CHAPTER 3

Working with an Attorney

Seven-thirty at night is not a time when most people seek out a fresh cup of coffee, but personally, I like to keep myself caffeinated! This is especially true on the weekends when I find myself working later than expected to keep up with my cases and make sure clients are taken care of.

It was on one of those Saturdays when I decided to finally leave the office and work from home for the rest of the evening. It was too late for Starbucks to be open, but there's a 24-hour coffee stand that's just a little bit out of my way home. I got in my car and started heading in that direction. My stomach rumbled. I debated whether I should go home and make dinner instead. That sounded like a smarter move. After being at the office all day, I really wanted to go home. But I felt an inexplicable draw toward the coffee stand. When I tell my friends this story, they laugh and say that I aways feel drawn toward coffee, but this time was different! It was like the universe was telling me I should go there.

I pulled up to the coffee-stand window and the young barista immediately started chatting me up. He asked me what I do for work, and I told him I am a personal injury attorney. His eyes got huge, and he said he had been praying for God to bring him a new attorney. I got goosebumps. He told me he had been hit by a car while walking down the street and been severely injured. He had hired an attorney who got him a low six-figure settlement offer, but he didn't think it was enough. "I could have died," he said.

Given the extent of his injuries, the settlement offer didn't sound like enough to me either. His medical bills alone were almost in the six figures already, and he was still on the road to recovery.

A general rule of thumb is to multiply one's medical bills times three to be in the ballpark of a fair settlement. This rule can, however, dramatically change from case to case—and for severe accidents such as this one, I believe that injured people should get even more.

The barista expressed to me that his attorney was pressuring him to take the deal and was also impossible to get a hold of. I let him know that I thought I could get him significantly more money—and that I always call my clients back. He decided to transfer his case to me.

Over the next nine months, my team and I worked hard to compile all the evidence we needed to show that the settlement should be significantly higher. Our client had sustained severe injuries, and his life would truly never be the same. The at-fault driver's insurance company was trying to minimize this reality, which was a morally corrupt thing to do. Personally, it irks me when big companies refuse responsibility for taking care of victims. It's just wrong. After all, the whole purpose of insurance is to help people when they need it. That's why we felt compelled to fight for this client as he struggled to ease back into what anyone could reasonably call a "normal" life. My team and I put the time in going back and forth in numerous rounds of negotiation with the insurance company, inching our way closer to a fair number.

In the end, we got a settlement for almost a million dollars. You read that right. We were able to get about four times more than the client's original attorney thought he should settle for! It was a life-changing amount of money for my client and his family.

Outcomes such as this are always satisfying to hear about because they show that there can indeed be a light at the end of the tunnel for victims of car accidents. At the same time, it's also a little scary to hear how people experience vastly different settlement outcomes based solely on negotiation strategies. In this chapter, I want to break this down, as it gets to the heart of everyone's greatest fear after they've been in an accident: getting much less than they deserve.

Fees

Let's start out by addressing fees, because that's the first thing a lot of people worry about. If lawyers were 100-percent free, everyone would hire them. But that isn't the case. Attorneys are known for charging hundreds of dollars an hour, and the work that's required can quickly drive up the number of billable hours. Many car-crash victims question whether this kind of expense is worth it in the long run or if they would end up with more money if they represented themselves.

The first thing to know about working with a personal injury attorney is that we charge differently than just about every other type of lawyer. We don't do hourly billing, and we only get paid if our clients get paid. This is called working on a contingency fee. The standard industry rate is 33.33 percent of the total settlement, or 40 percent if a lawsuit is filed. This means that you don't have to worry about coming up with money to pay your attorney up front. And in the unlikely situation that you don't end up recovering any money in your case, you won't have to pay your attorney anything. This removes a big financial hurdle and an element of risk in seeking legal representation.

Now, you might be thinking that parting with 33.33 percent of your settlement means that you will receive less because your piece of the pie is smaller. But the reality is that attorneys almost always get their clients a pie that is many times larger than what they could expect to get on their own. This is true for cases that go to trial, as well as those that are settled out of court. One key reason for this is that attorneys have a good idea of how much their clients should be getting, and they understand how to negotiate with insurance companies to recover a fair settlement.

In the previous chapter, I mentioned that the national average settlement recovery without an attorney is $17,600. This could sound like an impressive amount, but after paying for medical bills and car repairs, you probably wouldn't break even. The national average settlement recovery with an attorney is $77,600. That is more than a 440-percent increase.[5] When you subtract the standard attorney's fee ($25,866.66), you're left with $51,733.33.

Which would you rather have? A whole small pie worth $17,600 or a big slice of pie worth $51,733.33?

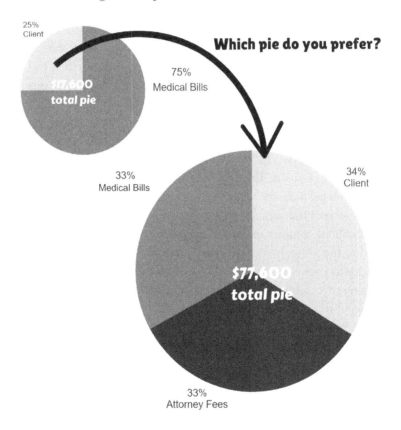

You might be wondering why victims get so much more money when they have an attorney represent them. The answer is simple: insurance adjusters know that they can't take advantage of attorneys. A lot of people consider themselves to be good negotia-tors. And many are! They can get a good deal when they're talking to a mechanic about fixing their car, or they're able to advocate for themselves to get a salary increase at work. But negotiating a per-sonal injury case is significantly different. If you aren't a licensed attorney, insurance companies simply will not take you seriously. They are well aware that you don't know how much your case is worth and that you don't even know the steps you need to take to file a lawsuit on your own. They will use that to their advantage every time they can.

Choosing the Right Attorney

It's easy to see that car-crash victims recover more money with an attorney than they do without. But going back to the case with the barista, it's more difficult to understand how car-crash victims can end up with wildly different settlement outcomes based on which attorney they choose to hire.

One reason the law is so complex is because no two cases are exactly the same. There is always a range of cir-cumstances that make each case unique. Because of that, there is never one "right" an-swer for how much a case is worth. Instead, it can be ar-gued in various directions.

> One reason the law is so complex is because no two cases are exactly the same. There is always a range of circumstances that make each case unique.

To further complicate the situation, it's impossible to remove the human element from the legal process. In every case, it's a hu-man negotiating with another human. And if those humans can't come to an agreement, other humans (e.g., a judge or jury) are selected to step in and help reach a resolution.

As you can imagine, this leads to a wide range of outcomes. Think of it as a bell curve. Given the type of case and general circumstances, most outcomes fall into a middle range. From there, cases fan out in either direction, with plaintiffs getting higher or lower settlements than the average.

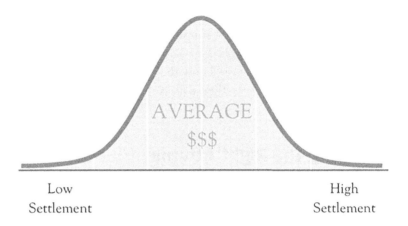

Low
Settlement

High
Settlement

Most attorneys try to get their clients higher-than-average settlements, but they might be viewing the circumstances through different lenses, which impacts the bell curve they are anticipating. It's also possible that the other parties involved in the case behave in unexpected ways, which can create surprising outcomes. In other words, it isn't an exact science.

Different Law Firms, Different Approaches

At my firm, I try to get my clients as much as I possibly can. I want to be on the far-right side of the bell curve. But I'll be honest: getting that kind of money isn't easy. Those are the cases that often end up being incredibly time-consuming and go on for many months, if not more than a year. Because they require so much of my firm's resources, we don't have the bandwidth to take on an unlimited number of such cases. Although I continue to incrementally expand my number of team members and offices, I don't want to take on more cases than we have the bandwidth to handle or to not give a 100-percent effort for our clients. I take this approach because it's where my passion lies. I know that, with enough hard work, I can get my clients the kind of life-changing settlements they deserve.

Not all firms are like this. I don't want to speak negatively about others, but the reality is that some of them take a different approach. Remember how attorneys get 33.33 percent of whatever their clients recover? Well, there are different ways to make the same amount of money. For example, on a case with a $1 million settlement, I would make $333,333. Considering all the time and effort I would put into a case of that magnitude and complexity, I could have taken 40 other cases that all had a $25,000 settlement and made the exact same amount. Or I could have taken 20 other cases that all had a $50,000 settlement. Or 10 cases that all had a $100,000 settlement. You get the idea.

When a victim is willing to accept less money, it's much easier and less time-consuming for the attorney and law firm to settle their case. That's why some firms use a volume strategy. They bring in as many clients as possible and try to settle their cases as quickly as they can. With this strategy, they "serve" many more people than other firms do, and the 33-percent fee for all the small settlements adds up. In the industry, these types of law firms are pejoratively referred to as "settlement mills." They exist in the left side of the bell curve, driving outcomes that are only slightly better than people who choose not to hire attorneys.

As a car-crash victim, you don't want to choose a settlement mill to represent you because they will not have your best interest at heart. They will want to settle your case as quickly as possible to get a little money in your pocket and a little money in their pocket and then move on to the next case. This works for them because it's a volume business and they can always make more money. But this is your only shot at recovering the funds you need to pay your medical expenses and make you whole. Your case deserves more time and attention than settlement mills would be willing to give.

So how do you know if a law firm is a settlement mill? A major red flag is any kind of messaging around how the firm will help get you money fast. When it comes to recovering what you truly deserve, speed is your enemy. It takes time to see how your body heals after an accident, and rushing that process could cause you to settle your claim for less than the value you deserve. The allure of fast cash is not worth it in the long run.

Another sign that a firm won't put in the extra time and effort for your case is their track record with how often they file lawsuits and how many of those cases actually go to trial (for more than $100,000) or arbitration. Sometimes insurance companies dig in their heels and refuse to offer a fair settlement. In those situations, the only way to get a reasonable outcome is by filing a lawsuit and preparing to go to court.

When you file a lawsuit, you're assigned a trial date about a year away. Preparing to go to court can take an enormous amount of work and require hundreds of hours of research, planning, and strategy. We delve deeper into this process in a later chapter, but in a nutshell, it's a lot of work for everyone involved—and many attorneys do not want to do it.

It can also be stressful for attorneys as they think about standing up in a courtroom in front of a judge and jury and putting everything on the line. For many of them, this is their least favorite part of their job. It can be hard for introverted people to speak in front of an audience, especially in a high-stakes scenario, and a trial is the ultimate high-stakes scenario. Not only do attorneys have to craft a compelling argument and present it in front of a room full of strangers, but they also have to be ready for another person to argue that they are totally, stupidly, ridiculously wrong. That's why so many attorneys absolutely dread going to court.

I get it. I really do. But shying away from going to trial doesn't create the best possible outcomes for clients.

Insurance companies pay attention to which law firms file suits and which see them through to completion instead of settling early. When attorneys have a track record of being less aggressive about going to court, insurance companies will offer them less money because they know they probably won't push for more because they don't want to go to court. (Remember: these are real people negotiating against other real people, and they will absolutely try to exploit the other side's weaknesses.)

Personally, I love going to court. It might sound crazy, but I look forward to those days! Being in the spotlight is where I thrive. I used to be a musician, and I always loved performing in front of crowds. Being in the courtroom gives me that same feeling—everything else disappears, and I am fully present in the moment and laser-focused on what I need to do. Since I enjoy trials so much, I don't hesitate to go in that direction whenever an insurance company refuses to offer a fair settlement to my client. Yes, the case becomes more work for my firm and the process takes longer, but it's worth it for my client when they walk away with way more money than what they ever thought they were going to receive.

When you're looking for the right attorney, you should always ask how they feel about going to trial and how often their cases go that route. It will tell you a lot about what you can expect in terms of how they will treat your case.

The Confusing Zone of Mediocrity

A lot of clients end up with a law firm that seems neither especially great nor particularly terrible. This can be confusing in itself. Maybe they receive an offer from the other driver's insurance company that isn't offensively low but doesn't seem high enough either. The law firm might pressure the client to take the deal. If the client isn't motivated to sign the paperwork, then the deal just sits there and the case stalls. I see this all the time. Attorneys and clients don't see eye to eye. The client wants more, but the firm either doesn't think it can get more or doesn't think it will be worth the extra time and work to get a higher settlement. These scenarios are tricky because clients aren't sure how well they are being served. I came across a situation like this recently in an unexpected way.

In addition to practicing law, I teach a law class at a local college. One of my students, Ali, was from Iraq, where he had been a licensed attorney. Upon moving to the United States, Ali's goal was to ultimately practice law here. Speaking English as a second language made this goal harder to reach, but I believed Ali could do it.

During that semester, he showed up at my law firm's office unannounced and asked if he could be an unpaid intern. I'd never hired an intern before, but I had witnessed Ali's passion and work ethic, and I knew he would do a good job. He started out doing coffee runs but quickly became a key person at our firm, helping on almost every case. He was observant and patient and offered good insight.

One day, he told me that he had been injured in a car accident about a year prior. He had hired a different attorney before he'd met me, and it seemed like the case wasn't going anywhere. His attorney was hard to reach, and very little progress had been made in months.

Ali saw how we take care of our clients, and he realized that we provide a totally different level of service. For example, we call our clients every single week to check in with them, regardless of what's currently happening in their case. That's because we want to know how their treatment is coming along and how they are feeling. Checking in proactively also allows us to see if clients have any new questions or need help with anything. This level of communication makes cases go smoother because it keeps everyone on the same page.

Although it's a best practice for us, most law firms don't operate like this. Many clients, like Ali, rarely hear from their lawyer during their case and consistently feel like they don't know what's going on. When a firm doesn't reach out proactively, clients feel like they are being a burden if they ask questions, so many don't and end up left in the dark not knowing what to do. This is where Ali was with the first attorney he had chosen.

After his stint working as an intern at our firm, he asked me if he could transfer his case to me to see if I could finally get him a fair settlement. I was honored that he wanted to switch—especially after getting a good look at how we really do business.

It took us a few months to negotiate the case, but we ultimately got Ali a six-figure settlement. Even though he had been in pain for a long time, he had no idea the case was worth that much. He was thrilled. In fact, he's become one of our biggest promoters and has helped us connect with the Iraqi Community Association, where we put on Know Your Rights events.

Although this case came to us in a unique way because Ali was our intern, my firm gets a lot of cases that had previously been handled by other firms. This is usually because clients aren't thrilled with their settlement offers. They are working with firms that are on the low-to-middle range of the bell curve—and they want to be on the high end. I don't blame them; that's what I wanted when I was in a severe car accident. It takes more time and effort for attorneys to fight for settlements that do their clients justice, but I believe it's worth it.

As a car-accident victim, you should never feel like you have to settle for mediocrity. If you're ever in a situation where you are starting to feel that way, it's time to look for a new law firm.

Statute of Limitations

When you get in an accident in Washington state, you have three years to either reach a settlement agreement out of court or file a lawsuit. After that, you're unable to get any compensation, regardless of how severe your injuries were. Be very careful regarding the statute of limitations. It varies in length from state to state. For instance, the statute of limitations in Oregon is only two years. Your attorney can advise you regarding this.

I would never recommend waiting anywhere near that long to get representation from an attorney. That said, it's funny how many people call my firm at the eleventh hour, right before their statute of limitations expires. Almost all of them have already received a settlement offer or two from the other driver's insurance company, but they have a hunch that they should be getting more. They keep this deal in their back pocket, and months turn into years, until finally a week or two before their deadline, they consider hiring an attorney—or transferring the case to a law firm that isn't mediocre.

Many attorneys—including a lot of good ones—will not take these cases on because they are too much work at the last minute. As an attorney, if you represent someone who is at the tail end of their statute of limitations and you don't get the paperwork filed on time, you can get a malpractice claim filed against you, which can create major problems for your license to practice.

Preparing the paperwork to file a lawsuit is not a simple task. A lot of people think it's just clicking a button. That is not how it works. It can take a couple full days of work, or longer, to gather the proper materials and draft the documents. Waiting until the eleventh hour makes this process stressful and risky.

If you were in an accident a while back and your statute of limitations is starting to wind down, do not delay deciding on how to move forward. The longer you wait, the fewer options you will have.

When it comes to picking an attorney to represent you, the decision isn't much different from evaluating any other potential relationship. Do they value you and your time? Do they seem like they have your best interest at heart? Do they demonstrate healthy communication standards? If yes, these are all good signs that you're making a smart decision. But if the answer to any of these questions is no, move on. There are plenty of attorneys in the sea, and there's no point in settling for someone who doesn't deserve to handle your case.

CHAPTER 4

Understanding Insurance Coverage

Most people don't fully understand what their auto insurance actually covers. Before I became a personal injury attorney, I was in the same boat! I bought insurance from a company that I had heard of before and believed to be reputable, and then I just guessed at the level of coverage I should buy, factoring in the price. I didn't want to waste money and buy more than I needed, but I was also worried about not having enough coverage if I were to get in a major accident. (Although I believed that—fingers crossed—it was unlikely to happen.) In the end, I relied on the insurance salesperson to help explain things. After I made my decision and bought the policy, I never thought about it again. Of course, I paid the bills to keep renewing, but I forgot all the details around the policy limits and what was covered.

Let's be honest: insurance is boring. Would you want to sit down and chat about insurance policies with a friend over coffee? Probably not. Buying coverage for hypothetical future accidents isn't really something most people like thinking about because they hope they'll never actually need it. Insurance is more of a legal hoop to jump through than anything else. You know you're legally required to have it, and getting it is the responsible thing to do, so you pick a policy and move on with your life.

This is the way the vast majority of drivers choose their insurance policies: it's an administrative task, not a major life decision.

As a personal injury attorney, I cannot tell you how many times I've worked with someone who would give anything to turn back time and choose a different insurance policy. What seemed like a fairly inconsequential decision turned out to be the difference between financial security and financial ruin. I wish that were an overstatement, but it's not.

After you've been injured in a car accident, your medical bills can be astronomical. We're talking in the tens of thousands, or even more. And if you're severely injured, you can no longer work. When you lose your paycheck, your family struggles to pay the bills. If the car that was destroyed in the accident was your family's only vehicle, there's the added stress and expense of finding new transportation. All the responsibilities you used to handle, from taking your kids to school to cooking meals to cleaning the house, now need to be done by someone else because you're physically unable to do them. And while your family members step up to try to earn more and take care of more around the house, they are also forced to take care of you as you recover. The burden this creates is life-changing. I see people go through it all the time, and it's a terrible situation to be in.

It's impossible to see into the future and know what kind of insurance coverage you will actually put to use, but I can tell you without a doubt that you are better off safe than sorry. Paying a little more each month to get a good amount of coverage is worth it.

One key reason for this is simple: about one in five drivers is uninsured. In Washington state alone, there are over a million of them on the roads. If one of those uninsured motorists runs into you, chances are that you will be getting exactly zero dollars from them. They'll get a $550 ticket for driving without insurance, which will be paid to the state, and you'll be left trying to figure out how to cover your hospital bills, buy a new car, and rebuild your life.

But if you have an insurance policy that includes the right types of coverage, you can recover money to pay your bills no matter who hits you.

Because insurance is so important, in this chapter, I break down exactly what you need to know. Stick with me. I realize this is nobody's favorite topic, but it's worth spending 15 minutes to learn the basics. Not only will this help you understand what kind of coverage you have now if you've been in a recent accident, but it will also help you decide whether you want to increase your current policy so that you're better covered in the future.

Policy Limits

The most important thing to understand about insurance coverage is the policy limit. This is the maximum amount that an insurance company will pay out for various damages and, thus, the most you will be able to receive from that company for your accident. There are a few types of policy limits:

- **Bodily injury max per person.** There is a maximum amount the insurance company will pay out to each person who was injured in the accident. In the state of Washington, you must have at least $25,000 in coverage.
- **Bodily injury max per accident.** There is a maximum amount the insurance company will pay out per accident. In the state of Washington, you must have at least $50,000 per accident. When accidents involve multiple people who were injured, the payout is likely to reach the max per accident before the max per person.

Note that these two policy limits are always bundled together at different levels. For example, your policy limits might be $25,000/$50,000 or $100,000/$300,000. Opting for more coverage means that the policy will be more expensive.

Here's how policy limits come into play after an accident:

- If you are driving alone in your car and someone hits you, and they only have the minimum legal requirement for insurance, you can get a max of $25,000 from their insurance company for your injuries.
- If that same person hit you and you had one passenger in your car, you can each get $25,000 for your injuries.
- If there were three people in your car, the limit is $50,000 total for all three people. Determining how that money should be allocated could get complicated. Rather than dividing it evenly, it would likely be based on the severity of each person's injuries.

Personal Injury Protection

Personal injury protection (PIP) provides at least $10,000 in benefits for any medical bills, regardless of who was at fault in an accident. Anyone can elect to add PIP to their insurance policy, no matter what insurance provider or policy they choose. One of the best things about PIP is that the money is paid out to the medical provider right away, which means they don't have to wait for your case to close to get paid for treating your injuries.

PIP was created in the 1970s as a result of so many people finding themselves unable to pay for medical bills after an accident, as insurance companies often try to deny liability of their insured driver, which drastically slows down the process of getting money to car-accident victims to cover their immediate medical expenses. Although PIP is a little different in every state, it's available nationwide.

In the state of Washington, you can forgo PIP coverage, but you will be required to sign a waiver. Personally, I think this gives good context for how important PIP is. If you have to sign a waiver in order to decline something, it's because you're choosing to take on some sort of risk. This is exactly what you're doing if you choose to not pay the extra $10–20 a month for coverage. The expense is extremely low when compared with the amount of coverage you receive. Opting to forgo that coverage is not a smart decision. That's why the insurance company makes you sign a waiver.

That said, if you go to an insurance salesperson and tell them you're broke and need the least-expensive option possible, they're going to tell you that you can opt out of PIP if you just sign on that dotted line. And if you haven't done your research to know that PIP is actually an amazing deal and could get you out of a very bad situation later, you might forgo coverage. That's why I'm here to tell you that you should always add PIP to your insurance policy even if you're struggling to make ends meet—no, *especially* if you're struggling to make ends meet. (If $10–20 a month seems like a burden, imagine having to come up with $10,000 to cover your hospital bills.)

You can find out whether you have PIP coverage by reviewing your insurance policy or getting in touch with your attorney or insurance provider. If you don't currently have PIP, have your insurance provider add it today. Just be aware: if you ever signed a PIP (or an uninsured motorist [UIM]) waiver, it will stay in force for the lifetime of that insurance policy, even if you sell your car and buy another one, assuming you maintain the same policy (which most often is the case). If you want to change that and purchase PIP/UIM coverage, you must advise your insurance company in writing that you want to void the previous waiver and purchase the PIP/UIM coverage. It's important to then also make certain you are being charged for that new coverage by reviewing your bill.

Lastly, if you are able to pay a bit more, you can opt to get extended PIP coverage, which can be $25,000 or $35,000 depending on the company. This is highly recommended.

Uninsured Motorist Benefits

Though this is often seen as an add-on, since it's not legally required for a minimum insurance policy, it's one of the most important decisions to make. That's because roughly one in five drivers is uninsured. That means there's a 20-percent chance you will be completely screwed without this coverage. Don't let this happen to you. Always opt for UIM coverage.

According to the National Highway Traffic Safety Administration, the average cost of medical treatment for a minor car-accident injury is more than $15,000.[6] You can expect to pay even more if you are in an accident that requires hospitalization, surgery, rehabilitation, and other medical expenses. With that in mind, you should get at least that much in coverage. It might only make your policy go up a few dollars a month. And if you can afford more, get more! This is how you can best protect yourself and the people in your car. You can't control what other people do, but this is an area where you are able to get as much coverage as you want. If you often have family members and friends in your car, think about how much money it could realistically take to cover medical expenses in a major accident. I've worked on many cases where $25,000 in UIM was helpful, but the victim had tens of thousands of dollars they ended up having to pay out of pocket.

Just like PIP, it is a legal requirement in Washington that all insurance companies offer you UIM, and you need to sign a waiver to decline. I've had a couple of cases where my client didn't have UIM on their policy, but the insurance company couldn't find the waiver they signed declining coverage (likely because they were never given the waiver in the first place). Without the signed waiver, the insurance company is required to offer the lowest level of UIM coverage FOR FREE. Get your attorney's help with this one, and make sure you elect to have UIM moving forward.

Excess UIM Umbrella Coverage

Another smart option for insurance is umbrella coverage, which offers protection over and above your auto and homeowner's policies. Experts I have spoken with say that the recommended minimum policy limit a person should consider is $1 million. Having a policy such as this in place is the best way to protect yourself and your family, since you can't control what kind of policies other people have. And if you get into an accident where someone sues you, this is the type of policy that you'll be thankful you have.

Special Circumstances

Certain scenarios can impact your insurance coverage and/or claim in a major way. If any of these circumstances apply to your accident, make sure you explain them to your attorney from the onset of working with them.

- **Driving for work.** If you're injured while driving for work, it's possible that you might be looking at a worker's compensation claim rather than a personal injury claim. There are nuances to this, and it can depend on the nature of your job, including whether you were clocked in or on break, whether you were between runs, or whether you were on a trip for work. It's also possible that you could get both worker's comp and a personal injury settlement. You would need an attorney to review your case to know for sure.

- **Uber / Uber Eats / Lyft.** If you are a rideshare passenger and injured in an accident, it doesn't matter who was at fault. You still have a case. But if you are a rideshare driver, it's different. A regular insurance policy might not cover you during times when you're driving for work. In fact, I've seen instances when an insurance company knew that someone worked as a rideshare driver and then go out of their way to try to prove that the person was working when they were injured because that would disqualify them from a settlement. And the insurance company has the right to request time slips and other details during an investigation—if it asks for them. If you're a rideshare driver involved in an accident, my best advice is to talk with an attorney immediately. Beware of oversharing with police, and ideally don't talk to the insurance companies that are involved without first consulting an attorney.

- **Driving someone else's car.** Coverage can vary, so make sure you check the details. Depending on the policy, it might cover the individual driver or anyone driving the car who had permission from the policy holder. Also double-check the details for any adult children who are on their parents' insurance but don't live in the same household, as the insurance company may refuse to cover them.

- **Rental cars.** If you have your own car insurance and you rent a car, your regular policy will carry over for bodily injury. The rental-car company will offer to sell you additional insurance, but this is primarily for property damage, and it's not required. However, if you don't have any car insurance, you will need to purchase it as an add-on from the rental-car company. Otherwise, you will be driving as an uninsured motorist.

- **Expired driver's license.** You might get a ticket for "no valid operator's license" (NVOL), but it will not affect your ability to collect money on a personal injury claim.

- **Suspended license.** Driving with a suspended license is a misdemeanor, and penalties can include jail time. However, doing so will not affect your ability to collect money on a personal injury claim. Licenses often get suspended due to financial reasons, such as unpaid court fees or not paying child support. If you are in this boat, resolving your personal injury case could be what you need to break free from a downward financial spiral.

Getting Affordable Car Insurance

Most people know that insurance can be more expensive depending on both the type of car you drive and your driving history. But did you know that people pay different amounts for the exact same insurance coverage from the exact same company? It's unfair but true. Insurance companies often use a tiered pricing system that is broken into what they call a "preferred market" and a "standard market." When you apply for coverage, they use your credit report to determine which category you fall into. People who are higher earners and have higher credit scores are offered the preferred rate, which is generally 18 to 20 percent cheaper than the standard rate. Unfortunately, if you have bad credit or collections on your record, you are likely to be offered the standard rate and pay more for the same coverage. Most insurance brokers are not in control of what their company offers individual customers, and they don't explain how differences in pricing are based off the customer's financial history.

I spoke with a representative from Farmers Insurance, and she is passionate about helping people get good insurance they can afford. She loves working with her clients to help them get the best possible rate for their policy. She says that many people have mistakes on their credit history that are causing problems with their credit report. Victims of fraud and identity theft also struggle with getting approved for lower rates. Fixing these issues on a person's credit report can make a huge difference in how much they have to pay for car insurance. You can learn more from my podcast, *Iron Mind,* at www.ironmindpodcast.com or on any streaming platform.

Iron Mind Podcast

Jordan's Story

Long ago, before I was the go-to guy for car accidents, I got a call from my friend Jordan's mom. Jordan and I had been friends since we were kids. He was known by all our friends for being the nicest guy around. He followed his passion for culinary arts and became a chef, and we all benefited from his love for baking. Jordan had recently gotten married to an amazing woman, and he was living the life he always wanted.

Although I knew Jordan's mom, I was surprised to hear from her out of the blue. Immediately, I knew something was wrong. She told me that Jordan had been in a bad car accident on the freeway. The doctors were saying he was paralyzed from the neck down and fighting for his life.

As Jordan's family gathered by his bedside, they started wondering about his hospital bills. The accident wasn't Jordan's fault, so the other driver's insurance should cover his expenses, right? They soon found out that the other driver only had the minimum coverage, which was basically used immediately upon entering the hospital. After racking up six figures in expenses over several weeks, Jordan's family had to worry about how he would get around at home in a wheelchair. They would have to renovate the house to make it wheelchair accessible, which would be a big expense and a major undertaking.

I remember talking with Jordan when he was trying to settle back into a normal life at home, and things were rough. He cried to me on the phone about how this wasn't the life his wife had signed up for, and on top of that, they were going to be in so much debt that they wouldn't be able to crawl out. In that moment, I felt powerless. I wanted nothing more than to make things better for my friend.

Months went by, and Jordan continued to have health complications from the accident. There always seemed to be something that was getting worse instead of better. In 2023, Jordan got an infection from his port. And just like that, he passed away at 34 years old.

Time has gone by, and I still think about Jordan almost every day. He truly was the nicest guy. I know people always say that when someone dies, but with Jordan, it's true.

I don't necessarily think that having better insurance coverage would have changed anything about Jordan's health outcomes. But it definitely would have made his time after his accident much less stressful.

Jordan's experience made me understand the importance of properly preparing for things I hope will never happen. That includes buying the more expensive insurance policy that I hope I'll never have to use. That is what I recommend for all my clients. As an attorney, I do my best to get car-accident victims the money they need to cover expenses and more for their pain and suffering. But I can only get as much as the maximum policy limit. Sometimes, the policy limit is far below what my clients need or deserve. Those situations are awful. Don't let this happen to you. Check your insurance policy today and make sure you have enough coverage.

CHAPTER 5

What to Know When You're Injured

When you've been injured in a car accident, there is a liability component that puts you in a different situation than when being injured in other ways. You have the opportunity to get a settlement that can cover your medical expenses and compensate you for pain and suffering, disfigurement, impact on your ability to enjoy life, etc. But getting what you deserve will take time and effort.

I've already told you how important it is to seek medical care immediately after an accident, but I'm going to say it again: make sure you see a licensed physician within 48 hours of your accident. If

> *I'm going to say it again: make sure you see a licensed physician within 48 hours of your accident.*

you fail to do this, it will be much easier for the other driver's insurance company to argue that your injuries were minor or nonexistent.

But that's just your first step in addressing your injuries. In this chapter, I cover other things you need to consider when it comes to both your recovery and preparing yourself to obtain the maximum settlement that your injuries support.

I'll start by painting a picture of what most people do when they've been injured in a car accident. Let's call this example person Joe.

Joe is driving along the highway to work one morning when a car pulls out right in front of him. Luckily, he is wearing his seatbelt, and he isn't speeding. The crash is scary, but it's over quickly. When the dust settles, he's immediately grateful to be alive. He moves his arms and legs and fingers and toes, and everything is still working.

His attention shifts to his car, which is totaled. He loved that car, and it's the only one his family has. He immediately worries about how he will get to work in the coming weeks and how his family will get around.

Joe gets out of the car and notices that his lower back hurts, but that happens to him from time to time. An ambulance arrives at the scene and the paramedics examine him but determine that he doesn't need to go to the emergency room. They tell him to see a doctor within the next couple days to make sure he doesn't have any injuries that require treatment. Joe nods in agreement, but at the same time realizes he probably won't end up going. He's banged up a little, but it's nothing that some ice and ibuprofen can't handle. Besides, he doesn't have great health insurance and there's no point in wasting money just to have a doctor tell him to rest up.

Over the coming weeks, Joe deals with getting a rental car and then buying a new used car. His back hurts more than usual, but he pushes through, even going to the gym twice a week like he did before the accident. He posts a couple photos of himself at the gym to show his friends and family that he's doing well after the car accident. In the caption, he writes, "Almost back to 100%!" He isn't quite sure if that's true, but he doesn't want people to worry about him. When his wife had posted photos of their car after the accident, everyone had said that he was lucky to be alive.

He notices that his left fingertips feel tingly on and off throughout the day, but it isn't painful, and it doesn't bother him too much. It's not in his nature to make a big deal out of it, and he figures it will go away soon anyway.

Weeks turn into months, and Joe starts to feel like he's aging at warp speed. Everything aches when he wakes up. His back pain has become so bad that he's taking ibuprofen every day and can no longer lift weights at the gym. His knees hurt when he takes the stairs, and a couple of his fingers are now constantly numb. He starts to wonder if the car accident had impacted his body more than he realized at the time.

So many of my clients are like Joe. They're busy, hardworking people who don't want to make a fuss over themselves. They push through pain, they show up to work when they're supposed to, and they're optimistic about their health and recovery.

These are all great qualities to have, but when you've been injured in a car accident, this attitude will ruin your chances of getting the settlement you deserve. If you happen to be a doctor, you'll have the advantage of better understanding the full scope of your injuries. But if you aren't, you'll truly have no way of accurately assessing the state of your body after a crash. You would be shocked at how many times I've seen someone who had a symptom that seemed totally random only to have a doctor explain how it was caused by their accident. The body is nothing if not complex.

In the next chapter, I dive into details on some of the most common types of injuries that result from car accidents. But for now, let's focus on the main things you need to know about being injured in general.

Here's a summary of the process you can expect:

- See a licensed physician.
- Get a treatment plan.
- Undergo treatment.
- Assess progress.
- Adjust treatment as needed.
- Reach maximum medical improvement. (This term refers to the state of your body being the most improved it can be after your accident, which may or may not be the same as your pre-accident condition.)
- Settle your case.

This process can take many months, a year, or even longer—yes, it's a slow process. But if you try to speed it up, you will risk moving forward without gaining a full understanding of your injuries and will likely end up getting undercompensated.

During every step of this process, you should stay in regular communication with your lawyer's case manager. Keep them up to date on your treatment and your recovery. Ask questions and share any concerns you have. Your attorney knows that details matter in every case, and they will want you to keep them in the loop on how you're doing.

Five Key Considerations When You're Injured

1. Perception matters

The other driver's insurance company will try to minimize your injuries. They'll hire people who are incredibly thorough and whose job it is to analyze all your actions after the accident. That's why it's so important to get into the mindset that perception matters.

A lot of people like to work out—even after they've been injured. Many of them consider it a stress-relieving activity, and they try to figure out exercises that avoid the parts of their body that are in pain. A doctor is the best person to consult on whether this is a good idea from a health perspective, but from a legal perspective, I can tell you it could be problematic if you exercise in a public space. Insurance companies love to show footage of people exercising to claim they are faking injury.

It is important to be aware of this common insurance tactic if it applies in your case. For example, if you go to a gym where you swipe a card to get in or sign up for classes on an app, the insurance company can pull the attendance records and see all the times you've worked out. They can then request the camera footage from the gym to see what your mobility looks like. Unless you're staggering around and taking long breaks to massage your aching body, it's going to look like you're not that injured.

You also need to think about your online presence and how that can affect the perception of your injuries. If you go on that snowboarding or hiking trip after your accident and post about it on social media, it will be easy for an insurance adjuster to argue that you're not injured—even if your body hurt the whole time during your trip because of your injury.

If your account is private, count on them checking your friends' and family members' accounts to see if they can catch you doing anything active that they can hold against you as evidence of your good health. In these situations, it becomes harder for your attorney to give a strong argument on your behalf, and you are likely to get less compensation.

Pulling back on physical activity after a car accident is often one of the hardest parts of the process. I once worked with a former body builder who had been advised by his doctor to take it easy and rest after his accident. He said he felt like he was going crazy without lifting weights. But going to the gym meant jeopardizing his recovery and risking tens of thousands of dollars that he needed to cover his medical bills. He felt stuck between a rock and a hard place for almost a year. His mental health suffered as he lost the muscle mass he had worked so hard to achieve. Even though he was following doctor's orders, he felt like he'd lost his identity and the main thing that brought him joy. It got pretty dark for a while, but I told him to remember that this was a temporary situation and a means to an important end.

When you're injured, it's imperative that you work with your healthcare providers to get guidance on the types of physical activities you can participate in, especially as it relates to strenuous activities and exercise. You must also keep meticulous records on how these activities made you feel both while doing them and in the following several days afterward (e.g., Did the movement make you feel better or worse? How does this compare to how you felt before the accident? And how does the level of exertion compare to what you were doing before the accident?). Stay in close contact with your healthcare team to share your results and get their feedback for making any changes. Document all this because details and nuance matter. That way, if the other driver's insurance company obtains evidence that you were partaking in physical activity, you have the proper documentation that you were following doctor's orders for healing your injury.

And just to point out the obvious, it simplifies your case if you, your attorney, and your healthcare providers don't have to go down the route of addressing any strenuous physical activity after your accident to the other driver's insurance company in the first place. Consider being conservative, careful, and discrete.

2. Preexisting conditions matter

Make sure to tell your attorney about all preexisting health conditions you have—even it's from a slip-and-fall from 30 years ago. If your case goes to litigation, the other driver's insurance company will be able to see all past medical records, and you can be certain they are going to look for preexisting conditions and prior injuries. They can latch onto that information and argue that your injuries aren't new. It's best if your attorney is prepared for this.

That said, just because you have a preexisting condition doesn't mean that you're out of luck for getting covered. In fact, it's often the case that people with preexisting conditions need the most help after an accident. When your body isn't at 100 percent and you endure a car crash, chances are that things are going to get worse. (I've never seen a car crash magically heal a bad back, but I've seen many crashes make a bad back even worse.)

Seeking medical treatment after your crash will help you document how any preexisting conditions have changed over time. This can include your overall level of pain, how often you feel pain, and whether the new injury is causing new symptoms. When this is paired with diagnostic tests, such as MRIs or X-rays, you can build a strong case around how a crash has made an old injury worse.

We have a client who has been in five—yes, *five*—car accidents. And he's not even an Uber driver! He's just had some tough luck on the road. But one thing that has gone in his favor is that he has been good about going to the same doctors after each accident. They have been able to document all his injuries well and tell a complete story of his health, enabling us to show that he did in fact have new health complications from the most recent accident and that his pain was not from past accidents that could be considered preexisting conditions. This is a good example of how much documentation matters in an injury case.

3. Seniors are at heightened risk

As we age, our bodies change. Older folks who are going through degenerative aging are the most at risk for sustaining serious complications from minor accidents.

A client of mine named Raul was in a car accident when he was 63 years old. The car didn't have significant damage, so the accident seemed like no big deal. Raul's back hurt, but he thought he could recover just from seeing a chiropractor and getting some massages. He was with another law firm at the time, and no one ever talked with him about needing to see a licensed physician and get a treatment plan.

The other driver's insurance company was minimizing the accident, and his firm encouraged him to settle for the amount that was offered. Raul considered it and thought that maybe they were right, but his back still hurt. Finally, he saw a doctor and learned that he actually needed surgery, which he opted not to get. He also turned down the settlement offer. A couple years later, the pain still hadn't fully gone away.

He came to my firm to get a second opinion on his case, and he also got a second opinion from a different doctor. It turned out that the pain in his back was from a serious lumbar issue. In fact, he ended up needing a lumbar laminectomy, in which part of his spine would be cut out so his spinal cord could breathe a little better.

Although the body damage to his car had been minor, the body damage to his actual body was severe. This is not uncommon—especially for older folks. Luckily, the law helps protect people who are at heightened risk of injury. Referred to as "eggshell" victims, it is acknowledged that some people are more fragile than others and that minor accidents can have major complications that must be taken seriously. Seniors often fall into this category.

If you're in your golden years, know that injuries are more likely to become serious. Make sure you aren't dismissing your pain just because your car wasn't totaled. Health doesn't always just bounce back like it once did, and it's important to get a clear picture of this before your case is settled so that your attorney can get you the compensation you are entitled to and you don't undermine the value of your claim.

4. Getting injured again will complicate your case

If you're injured in a car accident and get hurt again before your case is settled, it's likely to complicate things. This is true whether you're in another car crash, you trip down the stairs, or you hit a tree while you're bicycling.

The other driver's insurance company is looking for reasons to minimize your settlement, and adding another injury will only buttress their claim. They can argue that all your significant injuries were a result of the second accident, not the first. With this reasoning, they will say that any pain or treatment that occurred after the date of the second injury should not be included in your case. It's possible to dispute this, but it can get murky. That's why it's best to be conservative and not take on any extra unnecessary physical risk. Pushing yourself to become more active and strengthen your body is not necessarily a bad thing. Just make sure you do so in conjunction with your medical provider's or physical therapist's recommendations.

5. Don't worry about paying for treatment

A lot of people worry about paying medical bills right after a car crash—especially when they learn that it can take many months or even years to settle a case. The good news is that you shouldn't need to pay any substantial healthcare bills immediately. When you have a good attorney who has experience handling personal injury cases, they should be accustomed to speaking with treatment providers and making sure you aren't pressured to pay bills before your case is resolved.

As an example, my clients' treatment providers can send a letter of protection to my office, and I can verify that their bills will be paid promptly upon receiving any settlement money. From then on, instead of sending bills to their patients, they hold onto them until the treatment is completed. This system works well for everyone. It helps my firm stay up to date on our clients' medical expenses, and it also protects our clients from the added stress of seeing bills come in that they can't currently afford. For providers, it gives them the peace of mind that their bills will be paid.

Keep in mind that your health insurance plan should also cover a portion of your medical expenses. If you have to pay any money out of pocket for your deductible or copay, you can get reimbursed at the end of your case when it's settled.

It's essential to note one caveat here: you should know what your insurance policy limit is so that you understand how much medical treatment is available to you. When you know what can be covered, you'll be more likely to get the treatment you need to fully recover. That said, the state of Washington, like many other states, is a "non-disclosure state," which means insurance companies are not required to share individual policy limits. This law has been put into effect under the guise that victims and personal injury attorneys will inflate claims and overtreat injuries based on that information. In reality, when people don't have this information, they are much more likely to minimize their injuries and treatment so that they don't end up with whopping medical bills they can't afford.

When policy limits are low, such as $25,000, and it's clear that treatment will easily exceed the maximum, insurance companies will share the policy limit information quickly and candidly, writing a check for the full amount right after the dust settles from the crash. But when policy limits are high, it's a totally different ball game.

At my firm, we make it a point to always find out the policy limits. Other firms will not always do that because it takes extra time and effort. This is a major differentiator in the level of service my firm provides compared with other firms in this industry. We work on uncovering this information early on in your case so that we know how much treatment can be covered and you don't have to worry about footing any unexpected bills.

Remember that you will not end up with more settlement money at the end if you forgo treatment. On the contrary, you are likely to end up with less, on top of not getting the care you need.

Your health is your greatest asset. To set yourself up for a solid recovery and to maximize your settlement, make sure you pay attention to these key considerations.

CHAPTER 6

Types of Injuries and Treatment

In this chapter, we delve into the most common types of injuries in car accidents and the symptoms to watch out for when you're hurt. By recognizing symptoms early on, you can prevent complications for your health—and your case—down the road. From whiplash to fractures, concussions to soft-tissue injuries, we explore the signs and symptoms that indicate you need medical attention.

My goal for this chapter is to help you feel empowered when it comes to your health and recovery. I want you to be able to communicate effectively with your doctor, ask good questions, and understand what to expect throughout the recovery process. It is important that you describe your symptoms accurately and ask informed questions in order to effectively work in collaboration with your healthcare team to help ensure that you get the right diagnostic tests and the care you need from the best possible specialists. Whether it's physical therapy for a sprained ankle or cognitive rehabilitation for a concussion, understanding your options empowers you to actively participate in your recovery.

The process of navigating medical care can be complex and time-consuming, so my firm offers a range of resources to our clients. We always prefer their treatment to be guided by a licensed medical practitioner rather than by us. And during our many years working in this industry, we have gotten to know a wide variety of providers throughout the state of Washington who accept many different types of health insurance carriers and plans. If you need help understanding a treatment plan from your PCP or scheduling appointments for the treatment modalities that align with a plan, we can help with that too. When it comes to receiving the best possible treatment and achieving optimal recovery, we're in your corner. It's this level of dedication you should seek out in the law firm you hire.

Common Types of Injuries

After working with hundreds of clients over the years, my team and I have seen the same types of injuries over and over again. They aren't always easy to recognize. In the following section, you'll find basic information on some of the most common types of injuries that result from car accidents—and signs for you to start identifying these injuries.

Soft-Tissue Injury

If you're in pain immediately after a car crash, you can pretty much guarantee that you have a soft-tissue injury. Bruises, sprains, and strains all fall under this category. All these can be fairly minor, but the challenge is in realizing whether your injuries might be more severe. The only way to know for sure is to see a licensed physician and, if necessary, get a treatment plan. Yes, it's possible that you might only need some therapeutic massages and a couple trips to the chiropractor, but that still counts as an injury, and you're entitled to get your treatment covered. You could end up getting all your massages covered and being compensated for missing work and also for any pain and suffering. And if your injury turns out to be more than just soft tissue, you'll know sooner because you'll have gotten a diagnosis from a doctor as well as documentation that shows when the pain started. If you are still experiencing pain after a few months of treatment, getting an MRI is one way to prevent intervening accidents or injuries from interfering with your car-accident claim down the line.

Broken Bone

This can be a major consequence from a car crash. Over the years, I've seen a ton, with some of the most frequent injuries being breaks to the sternum, ribs, spinal vertebra, clavicle, and pelvic bones. These fractures can occur when a person lurches forward sharply into their seatbelt. Breaks to facial bones, including the jaw and orbital, are also common due to the strike of an airbag or steering wheel.

A broken bone seems straightforward, but it's not always properly diagnosed. If you have swelling, bruising, or tenderness near an impacted area, you should get an X-ray immediately. But keep in mind that small bone cracks aren't always apparent in an X-ray—especially right after an accident—so you might need a follow-up X-ray later. It can take a couple days for a crack to fill with blood, which makes it more visible and easier to identify in an X-ray.

Hairline fractures are another injury that is difficult for doctors to diagnose. Without the proper treatment, a small crack in the bone can continue to expand, causing complications down the road.

With all this in mind, you can see why it's best to get checked out right after an accident and to continue advocating for yourself if you have any new or worsening symptoms in the days and weeks after your crash.

Traumatic Brain Injury

Also known as TBI, a traumatic brain injury occurs when the head or body goes through a violent impact or jolt. A case of whiplash or a mild concussion may only cause minor, temporary damage, whereas a severe TBI can lead to long-term health complications or even death. One important thing to note is that *you don't need to hit your head or be knocked unconscious to get a TBI*. It can result from any sort of movement where your body jerks hard enough that your brain sloshes inside your head and makes contact with your skull. This can cause bruising, swelling, and a range of known complications that doctors and scientists are still working to fully understand. And if you've ever had a concussion, you are more susceptible, and more likely, to have another one.

Severe TBIs (when people are knocked unconscious) are typically diagnosed quickly after an accident because people are taken by ambulance to an emergency room and are given proper diagnostic testing and a treatment plan. Mild to moderate TBIs are often more difficult to identify because the symptoms can take days, weeks, or even months to show—and they are often mistaken for other conditions. Over the years, I've seen a higher number of mild to moderate TBIs get misdiagnosed or not diagnosed at all. Folks with these types of injuries are often able to go about their normal lives and continue working or going to school, but over time, they just don't seem like themselves. They might have mood swings, irritability, and difficulty understanding what's happening in the world around them. They are often impulsive, lack restraint, and have trouble concentrating. On top of this, depression and anxiety are common, along with memory impairment and changes in sleeping patterns. Considering this vast range of symptoms, TBIs can be incredibly debilitating for people.

TBIs are even more difficult to diagnose and manage in children because they are often unable to explain their physical symptoms or sensory problems as well as adults. Adult caregivers must be vigilant in the days and weeks after a car accident to take note of any changes in a child's sleep habits, eating or nursing habits, or loss of interest in favorite toys or activities. If a child becomes unusually irritable or cries more often, these can also be signs of a TBI.

If you notice any of these symptoms in yourself or someone who has been in a car accident, make sure you or they speak with a licensed physician. A general practitioner will be able to refer a neurologist for testing.

Spinal-Cord Injury

Your spinal cord represents half of your central nervous system. Damage to its nerve fibers may interfere with or prevent communication between the brain and the rest of the body. This is how people become paralyzed and lose all feeling and mobility in parts of their body.

Some spinal-cord injuries don't result in paralysis, with people retaining some sensation or movement. They might experience tingling in the arms, legs, or feet, or radiating pain down the buttocks or legs. Other symptoms include difficulty standing or walking, intense pressure in the head, neck, or back, loss of bladder or bowel control, weakness, or loss of sensation in any part of the body.

Spinal stenosis happens when the space inside the backbone is too small. This can put pressure on the spinal cord and nerves that travel through the spine. Spinal stenosis occurs most often in the lower back and the neck. Some people with spinal stenosis have no symptoms. Others may experience pain, tingling, numbness, and muscle weakness. Symptoms can get worse over time.

The most common cause of spinal stenosis is wear-and-tear changes in the spine related to arthritis. People who have severe cases of spinal stenosis may need surgery. Surgery can create more space inside the spine. This can ease the symptoms caused by pressure on the spinal cord or nerves. But surgery can't cure arthritis, so arthritis pain in the spine may continue.[7]

This occurs most often in the lower back and neck. Symptoms generally start out minor and get worse over time. If you've exacerbated this type of injury as a result of your accident or you are at heightened risk for developing it, your best option is to take your time with treatment. This will enable you to get a full picture of the extent of your injuries, rather than settling before you realize how injured you truly are.

Herniated Disc

This is an extremely common injury, and you need an MRI to properly diagnose it. Unfortunately, MRIs, while being the most accurate diagnostic tool, are very expensive. That's why it isn't usually the first step in treatment recommended by a doctor. When a patient has back pain, they are often advised to try physical therapy first, or to work with a chiropractor or get therapeutic massages. After months of going this route and doing their best to manage symptoms, their doctor might order an MRI to confirm whether the patient has a herniated disc or just a soft-tissue injury, particularly if their symptoms include tingling, loss of sensation, and/or pain radiating down their arms or legs. Further treatment options include more invasive procedures such as steroid injections or burning of the nerves.

If you suspect that you might have a herniated disc, there's a good chance you will need to advocate for yourself. If you're experiencing intense pain or radicular symptoms, make sure your healthcare providers take you seriously and support you in taking the next treatment steps. Communicate with your lawyer to keep them in the loop on your pain and treatment.

Facet-Joint Injury

The joints along the spine can be damaged from the impact of a crash or the jarring movements that the body goes through in a collision. This type of injury can lead to long-term pain or immobility and usually requires chiropractic treatment and/or physical therapy. Victims must often wear a back or neck brace in order to straighten the spinal column and get the body back in working order. In more serious cases, spinal-fusion surgery could be an option.

Labrum Tear

This is a shoulder injury that results from a seatbelt doing its job in an accident—you don't go through the windshield, but your cartilage tissue tears. I see this a lot with taller people due to where the seatbelt hits their shoulder. This is the same type of injury that baseball pitchers and quarterbacks get from throwing a ball repeatedly. Symptoms can vary, but most people experience pain or an odd sensation that their shoulder locks up or slides out of place. Physical therapy can help, but if it doesn't, surgical treatment might be required to reattach torn ligaments to the bone. If your shoulder feels off after a car accident or you experience any changes in your range of motion, make sure you get it checked out.

Though this certainly isn't an exhaustive list of all the injuries you can sustain in a car crash, it covers the majority of the injuries I see from my clients. And of course, with all these conditions, some are more severe than others. I've noticed that some people are very lucky to walk away from serious accidents with minor injuries, whereas others have severe injuries from what was essentially just a fender bender. That's why it's so important to get checked out by a licensed physician and listen to your body. If you're in pain, make sure you communicate that to your doctor so that you can get the proper diagnostic tests and treatment. This is especially important when you would benefit from an MRI. An MRI is the best way to clearly see certain car-accident injuries:

- Spinal injuries
- Head and neck injuries
- Internal organ damage
- Joint inflammation
- Cartilage damage
- Nerve compression
- Torn or detached ligaments, tendons, and/or muscles

You often need to advocate for yourself so that your care team knows that you would benefit from an MRI. If you downplay your pain, you only make your condition more difficult to diagnose and treat properly.

It's also worth noting that being overweight or obese can increase your risk of injury. This is likely tied to the fact that crash-test dummies are made with an average BMI and motor-vehicle safety features are designed for and tested with bodies that are smaller than about two-thirds of Americans.[8] This can make a big difference in outcomes.

Treatment Modalities and the Impact They Have on Your Recovery Process

As a car-accident victim, embracing a diverse range of treatment modalities can significantly impact both your recovery journey and the potential value of your case.

Every injury, whether minor or severe, requires a tailored approach to treatment. Generally, I find that most people are familiar with going to a doctor, but many folks have limited experience pursuing other treatment paths, such as physical therapy. A licensed physician will be able to provide a treatment plan that considers these types of options, but it's always helpful when people come into the situation understanding the value of various treatment modalities so that they can advocate for themselves. For example, it's possible that your doctor might not suggest acupuncture as an option, but if you bring it up, they could quickly agree that it would make sense to give it a try. By incorporating a range of healing modalities, each with its own unique approach, you can achieve a more comprehensive, holistic, and balanced healing experience that drives better outcomes.

Here is a breakdown of some key treatment paths to consider as part of your wellness journey, possible benefits, and what to expect.

- **Physical therapy** focuses on restoring mobility, strength, and function through targeted exercises and techniques. It addresses musculoskeletal injuries, such as sprains, strains, and fractures, by improving range of motion, reducing pain, and enhancing overall physical resilience.

- **Chiropractic care** takes a holistic approach to spinal health, emphasizing the alignment of the spine and nervous system to promote optimal functioning of the body as a whole. Through adjustments, manipulations, and rehabilitative exercises, chiropractors aim to alleviate pain, improve mobility, and enhance the body's innate ability to heal itself.
- **Massage therapy** provides another dimension to holistic recovery by targeting muscular tension, promoting relaxation, and reducing stress levels. Beyond its physical benefits, massage therapy can also have profound effects on mental and emotional well-being, fostering a sense of calm, comfort, and connection with the body.
- **Acupuncture** is an ancient Chinese healing art in which needles are inserted into the body at specific points in order to promote healing. These needles increase blood flow, which aids in cellular repair and regeneration, while reducing inflammation. Improved circulation can help relax muscles and alleviate tension, naturally decreasing pain and promoting overall relaxation.
- **Mental health treatment** such as talk therapy can help with processing emotions after an accident. Many car-accident victims suffer from driving anxiety or post-traumatic stress disorder (PTSD), and talking with a mental health professional can make a big difference. With regard to experiencing a fear of driving following an accident, an experienced clinical psychologist can provide techniques designed to enable you to fairly quickly get over this type of anxiety.

Each type of treatment can contribute both a unique perspective and therapeutic benefits to support you on your healing journey. Make sure you talk to your doctor about what makes sense for your unique situation. I'd also advise you to keep an open mind when you start treatment. Going once or twice might not be enough to show you what you stand to gain from committing to regular appointments. If a doctor wants to see you three days per week, you should make every effort to comply with that treatment plan. If that frequency won't work for you, discuss it with the treating provider and they will work to accommodate a treatment schedule that fits your needs.

Taking a comprehensive approach to your recovery can also play a pivotal role in demonstrating the value of your case. Actively engaging in multiple forms of treatment shows a proactive approach to recovery, which is particularly important with severe injuries.

Just make sure that you have a reasonable balance when it comes to the types of treatment and that you're following a solid treatment plan. For example, physical therapy and chiropractic care are typically seen by insurance adjusters as being more legitimate and necessary forms of treatment than massage and acupuncture. That's why they like to see a larger portion of your treatment dollars going to a physical therapist or chiropractor than to a masseuse or acupuncturist. If this balance is out of whack, it can be a red flag that you aren't obtaining the treatment you need, and an insurance company will be more likely to push back against paying your bills. For example, spending $8,000 on massage and $2,000 on a chiropractor isn't a smart strategy.

Flaking out on your treatment appointments or slacking on your treatment plan is also a red flag to insurance companies that you aren't actually very injured. If you're supposed to be doing physical therapy every week for six months, you showing up once a month will hurt the value of your case. Make sure you are following the treatment plan you discussed with your doctor.

You always want to start with the least invasive treatment options to see what works. Many people start with chiropractic care and massage. Depending on what their physician recommends, they might try this route for a few months, and if things don't get better, they incorporate physical therapy. They try that for several months, and if it just isn't working, they opt for more diagnostic testing, such as getting an MRI.

If you find out you have a more serious injury, injections are another common treatment option. Here are some examples of how injections are used:

- Corticosteroid injections reduce inflammation and pain in both muscles and joints.
- Lidocaine injections provide pain relief by numbing an area of the body.
- Epidural injections treat pain in the lower back or legs.
- Nerve blocks are used to block pain signals from a specific nerve or group of nerves.
- Botox injections are most thought of for reducing wrinkles, but they can also be used to treat muscle spasms or chronic pain.
- Hyaluronic-acid injections help treat joint pain, such as in the knee or hip.

You should absolutely take this into consideration for your case. Injections can be scary if you don't know what to expect, but speaking with your healthcare provider can help you get the peace of mind you need to move forward.

If injections don't work, a more invasive option is to get radio-frequency ablation, a procedure that destroys the nerve fibers carrying pain signals to the brain. This treatment can provide lasting relief for chronic pain, especially in the neck, lower back, and arthritic joints, although frequently that relief may only last from 12 to 18 months, as the nerve ends regenerate. This is currently where I am with my neck pain from my car accident seven years ago. I've tried the majority of treatment modalities listed in this chapter, and although they've helped some, I still deal with moderate pain every single day. I'm hopeful that radio-frequency ablation will finally be the option that makes a real difference.

Malingering

When you fake or exaggerate an illness or injury to manipulate a situation and get what you want, it's wrong. It's what toddlers do when they say their legs hurt and they need you to carry them. It's also what some grown adults do when they want to get out of work, get an unneeded pain-pill prescription, or take advantage of an insurance company after an accident. Don't be a malingerer. Get the treatment you need, resolve your case, and be done with it.

Most people don't try to work the system for their advantage. However, enough people do it that insurance companies are always on the lookout for those who take advantage. This leads them to constantly misclassify car-accident victims as malingerers. It's helpful to know this so you aren't surprised when the other driver's insurance company tries to claim that you didn't need certain types of treatments. Don't waste your energy taking it personally and getting angry or defensive. This is just how insurance companies operate. They will always try to look for ways to argue that you deserve less money. Follow your doctor's advice, keep your law firm in the loop, and don't give the insurance company ammunition via social media to say you are a malingerer.

In the months following your accident, don't lose sight of the fact that your health is the most important thing to focus on—period. Yes, there will be competing priorities and times when you feel frustrated

> *Don't lose sight of the fact that your health is the most important thing to focus on—period.*

that your body isn't at 100 percent. Be patient and don't give up hope. The body has an amazing ability to heal. Put all your effort into getting better and see where it takes you.

A good law firm can help advise you during this process so that you get the treatment you need and also have the peace of mind that it will be covered financially. Your case manager should be regularly checking in to help assess your progress, address any concerns, and support you if your treatment plan needs to be adjusted. Maintain an open line of communication with your lawyer and healthcare providers, and continue advocating for yourself. Remember that you are not alone on your treatment journey.

CHAPTER 7

General Damages and Pain and Suffering

My client Tom was riding his motorcycle with his wife, Julie, on the back when a car pulled out right in front of them. They couldn't stop, and they were both thrown off the bike. Tom experienced a severe impact on his inner thigh up to his pubic bone. The tissue in that area was destroyed, including regions of his genitals. After seeing numerous specialists, including an excellent urologist, he still has no feeling in that area of his body.

Tom was in his 40s when the accident happened. Julie is about 10 years younger, and they had a five-month-old baby at home. They were just starting a family together and dreamed of having another child.

Julie was injured in the accident too. Even though she was experiencing constant pain herself, she ultimately had to stop going to her own treatment so that she could take care of her husband and infant.

The consequences of the accident quickly reverberated into other areas of their lives. Both Tom and Julie lost their jobs, and from there, they lost their house. They had to move in with Tom's mother, and the transition was not easy. Relationships became strained under these new circumstances. This often happens when roles change, and people are not used to spending so many hours caring for others or relying on others to care for them. Dreams that people once had are crushed, life loses its luster, and it's incredibly hard to move forward and get into a better spot physically, emotionally, and financially.

This is what pain and suffering looks like. It's not something people usually like to talk about, or even think about, but it's often a major aspect of car-accident cases.

In addition to your medical bills, there is value in your case both during and after you have completed the healing process. You might not get to 100 percent, and 90-percent healed is your new normal. Maybe you had an operation and now you just have to deal with aches and pains even though you have completed the surgical healing process. That 10-percent difference is a key part of your case. In the personal injury world, this gap is future pain and suffering, and it falls under the category of general damages.

There are many ways a person can be negatively impacted by an accident. When it involves a serious injury, there is often a butterfly effect that ripples through their life. Their new normal can be quite different from their old normal. As an attorney, it's my job to make sure that all these negative impacts are carefully considered when resolving a case.

Here's a list of types of general (non-economic) damages that should be considered as part of your case

1. **Physical pain and discomfort.** Beyond the immediate aftermath of an accident, victims may experience chronic pain that persists long after the injuries have supposedly healed. This can include continuous discomfort, limitations in movement, and the need for ongoing medication or therapy. The physical repercussions can affect every aspect of daily life, from personal care to the ability to work.

2. **Mental anguish and emotional distress.** The psychological impact of an accident can be just as debilitating

as physical injuries. Victims might struggle with anxiety that makes it difficult to get into a car or near traffic, depression due to changes in lifestyle and abilities, or severe stress from medical bills and lost wages. Sometimes people have relapses with alcohol or drug addiction, which only creates more problems. The emotional toll can also exacerbate physical recovery, fueling a vicious cycle of suffering.

3. **Loss of enjoyment of life.** This encompasses a person's diminished ability to enjoy some of the pleasures of life that had been part of a person's routine before the accident. It recognizes the impact of not being able to engage in activities that contribute significantly to an individual's happiness and well-being, such as sports, hobbies, or playing with children.

4. **Permanent disability or disfigurement.** Living with a permanent disability or disfigurement can profoundly affect a person's self-esteem, career prospects, and personal relationships. The compensation for such an injury seeks to acknowledge the subsequent lifelong challenges and necessary adjustments, including the mental health impact and need for modifications to living spaces and routines.

5. **Insomnia and sleep loss.** Chronic sleep issues following an accident not only affect physical health but also mental well-being. Lack of sleep can lead to irritability and decreased cognitive function and exacerbate mental health issues such as depression and anxiety, further hindering recovery and daily functioning.

6. **Reduced quality of life.** The cumulative impact of injuries, emotional distress, and the loss of life's pleasures can lead to a significantly reduced quality of life. This not only includes physical and emotional suffering but also the loss of independence, changes in personality, and the inability to perform daily tasks, maintain social relationships,

achieve personal goals, or engage in community or social functions.

7. **Future pain and suffering.** This acknowledges that the journey of recovery doesn't end with the conclusion of medical treatment. There may be future surgeries, long-term physical therapy, and other medical interventions required. Furthermore, the anticipation of living with chronic pain or the prospect of degenerative conditions developing as a result of the initial injuries can be a significant source of distress.

The butterfly effect of a serious injury can touch so many aspects of a person's life. That's a key reason why quantifying pain and suffering for compensation purposes can be complex. It requires thorough documentation, including medical records, psychological evaluations, and sometimes expert testimony. Attorneys also rely on previous jury verdicts and settlements from past cases to help put numbers to unique situations. But even then, we come across cases that are unlike anything we'd seen previously.

I once represented a woman who had been in a car accident when she was pregnant. She had a scheduled induction two weeks away and was looking forward to her husband coming home from his military deployment so he could be there for the birth of their first child. But after being in the accident, she was taken to the hospital and doctors said it was necessary to do an emergency caesarian section to get the baby out right away. The baby was born premature, and the dad missed the birth while serving his country. Thankfully, the baby and mother ended up being OK in the end, but it was incredibly scary and stressful for the whole family. Several people had to step in and help care for them while the dad was away.

The other driver's-insurance company didn't want to pay for pain and suffering in this case. The adjuster told me that the woman was "going to have the baby anyway" and she didn't see why it was such a big deal. That comment was enough to make us want to get litigious. Giving birth to a premature baby via emergency C-section while the dad is overseas is an incredible hardship. All the family members who were involved in the following weeks also went through hardship when they had to drop what they were doing and call off work to care for their loved ones. That's why we opened several claims against the insurance company for this accident. The baby had a claim. So did the mom, and the dad, and a few other family members. All their lives were negatively impacted as a result of the other driver's actions. Even if they didn't receive medical treatment for injuries, they were still affected by the negligence of the defendant. And that gets to the heart of what pain and suffering is about from a legal standpoint.

But how much is pain and suffering worth in dollars? When it comes to the law, there is no legal basis for coming up with a valuation. It's not like we can just use a guidebook to look up various injuries and compile an invoice. Since there is no such guide to consult (although if there were, it would certainly make things much more straightforward!), attorneys have developed various strategies for attempting to quantify the value of their clients' pain and suffering. This is important because when a case goes to litigation, there's a jury of people who don't know anything about putting dollar figures to hardship, and it's difficult for them to quantify without a little guidance.

One common way to put a valuation on pain and suffering is to multiply medical expenses by a certain number, which is usually three to seven. Thus, if a victim has $100,000 in medical expenses, an attorney might argue that they should receive anywhere from $300,000 to $700,000. From there, the attorney would explain why that number is appropriate.

Another common way to come up with a valuation is to assign a dollar figure to every day the victim has experienced hardship, as well as every day they are expected to do so in the future. With this method, actuarial tables are used to predict life expectancy, and the daily value is multiplied by the total days left. For example, in a recent case, I cited that the minimum wage in Washington state is $16.28 an hour. My client lost a lot of mobility in his accident, and he could no longer go hiking with his family or play with his kids. What's that worth every day? I argued that it should be worth at least two hours a day at minimum wage. He's 42 years old and, according to the nationally recognized actuarial table, was expected to live another 35 years and 77 days. At $32.46 per day, that's $417,175.92. I also wanted to factor in the months that had already passed since the accident, which added another $5,842.80. On a smaller scale, I've argued that a client's back pain from his accident should at least be worth the price of buying him a cup of coffee every day for the rest of his life. I multiplied $4 per day by 15 years and got $21,900.

Another method for evaluating pain and suffering from a car accident is by creating a life-care plan that quantifies continuing and current costs of care. This plan is created by an expert and includes a wide variety of expenses, such as medical equipment, future medical procedures, continuing medications, and the cost of household services they are no longer able to perform. Expenses are determined over the person's lifespan, factoring in expected inflation. A life-care plan also looks at lost earning capacity and how that factors into a person's finances. The total number is helpful to see because it shows where victims are expected to break even if they recover that dollar amount. For example, if the total is $500,000, recovering that amount is essentially getting nothing for pain and suffering. But using this multiplier method, an attorney might suggest that the victim deserves five times that amount.

Loss of Consortium

In addition to considering pain and suffering as part of the total value of your case, you should be aware of loss of consortium. This is typically related to the negative impact an accident has on a victim's relationships with their spouse, partner, parents, children, or other close family members. (These individuals do not need to have been in the car to make these claims.) The strain on relationships following an accident can be profound, including loss of support, companionship, and/or affection. Family members may find their roles drastically changed, having to act as caregivers or face the emotional burden of their loved one's suffering. Loss of consortium can be included in the same lawsuit as negligence, whenever appropriate.

Here are some examples of loss of consortium:

- The victim is injured in a way that no longer allows them to have sex with their partner, so the partner has a loss of consortium claim for how this has affected their intimacy.
- The victim has a TBI and their personality changes drastically. They become combative and hostile and yell at their mother all the time. The mother has a loss-of-consortium claim for how this has affected her parent-child relationship.
- The victim suffers from a shoulder injury and can no longer play catch with their son, a high school baseball player. The son has a loss-of-consortium claim for how this has affected their parent-child relationship.

It's easy for a jury to see how accidents can affect a victim's family members. That's why it's so important to identify loss of consortium at the beginning of your case. Make sure to discuss this with your attorney.

When it comes to putting a number to pain and suffering—or loss of consortium—there is no right or wrong amount. It's an incredibly difficult process, and what victims and their loved ones receive often varies depending on the situation and the individual judge or jury. But with all this ambiguity, one thing is certain: you need to understand the full scope of your hardship. That doesn't happen overnight. Thinking back to the butterfly effect of serious accidents, it takes months or even a couple of years for things to progress and for you to see the complete picture of what your new normal looks like. If you are able to reach 100 percent, that's a huge win! But if you aren't bouncing right back, take the time and effort to improve your health as much as you can before you resolve your case. It's possible that you might not reach 100 percent. But if that happens, and if you have a clear understanding of what your maximum medical improvement (MMI) is, your attorney can help define, assess, and evaluate the gap.

CHAPTER 8

Special Damages

Getting into an accident can be a hard hit to your wallet. From an ER visit to fixing your car to the paychecks you miss because you're laid up at home, the cost of being injured adds up quickly. That's a key reason to go down the legal path after being in an accident. In this chapter, we discuss what should be considered as part of the value of your case.

All the money you spend as a direct result of the crash, as well as the wages you miss out on earning, fall into what we call special damages. Unlike pain and suffering, special damages are quantifiable. When you have the documentation that verifies the expenses, such as receipts, statements, pay stubs, and bills, a good law firm will help you compile everything to create a full story of what the special damages look like for your case.

There are several key categories of special damages in the context of a car accident:

Medical and Rehabilitation Expenses

Often the lion's share of your expenses after an accident, medical costs include those for your hospital stay, surgeries, doctors' visits, prescription medications, physical therapy, and any other medical treatments that were needed as a result of the accident. There's a good chance you'll have so many bills that it may become challenging to keep track of everything. Do your very best to stay organized! Some people keep a Google/Excel spreadsheet to list expenses. Other people prefer the old-fashioned method of keeping receipts and paper bills in a folder or shoebox. Either way, if you start to feel stressed keeping track of these expenses, loop in a trusted loved one to help you. A bare-minimum best practice is to keep a running list of all the providers you see and all the places you go for treatment so that you don't forget to account for any expenses. The more treatment providers you visit, the harder it is to recollect where you went for treatment. Keeping track of where you go and reporting it to your lawyer in real time is the best way to ensure that nothing gets missed.

Lost Wages

If your injury caused you to miss work, you can claim the income you lost during that period. This is true for hourly workers, salaried employees, and those who are self-employed. No matter your line of work, your time has value. If you can't make it to work because of your accident, you are entitled to lost wages.

For salaried or hourly employees, if you use sick days or personal days to recover from your accident, the value of those days can be calculated using your W-2 or paystubs. If you took time off without pay, you can also claim lost wages for those days.

For contract workers and those who are self-employed, the process of determining the value of lost earnings can be a little more complex. Tax returns must be reviewed to gain a full understanding of the value of the time you were unable to work. For that reason, many firms don't dig into this area too much, and they often request significantly less than their clients deserve. When it comes to self-employed workers and those who receive 1099s, calculating special damages is an area where my firm excels. Before going into law, I was a master tax advisor. This financial expertise, paired with my understanding of the law, helps me fight for my clients so they can get the compensation they deserve.

Future Expenses and Reduction in Income

Even though the process of resolving your case can take months or even years, it's a good idea to anticipate that there may be more expenses down the road after your case is over. This happens regularly in car-accident cases with severe injuries, and there is a process for determining future special damages so that they can be included in your case and you'll be covered.

In those cases in which the potential damages are very significant, I typically engage a group of experts who work together through a specific process. To start, we hire a licensed physician (different from the doctor you've been seeing already) to do an independent medical evaluation. They review all your medical records, as well as internal notes made by your care team, and put together a report with their analysis on where you stand in relation to reaching MMI.

This report then goes to a vocational specialist who has expertise in the job market as well as how specific injuries can create limitations for employment opportunities. The vocational specialist compiles a report that paints the picture of your unique employment landscape. For example, if you are no longer able to work in the same type of role, could you still work in your industry? What other jobs might you be qualified for?

From there, this information goes to an economist, who plugs it into complex formulas to see what your finances look like relative to the marketplace now as well as in the future—either until you're expected to reach MMI or through the rest of your life expectancy. They then reduce the future impairment of earnings to a present value.

The next step is to gather all this information, along with any other evidence in the case, and share it with a life-care planner. This person has expertise in identifying long-term needs and costs after a life-changing injury. They are able to line-item a wide variety of expenses from vocational therapy to medical equipment to supplies to a home nurse and more. They also take into account other expenses that will arise from a change in your ability. For example, if you are no longer able to do laundry or mow the lawn, they will calculate the value of that through the duration of the limitation, be it for the next few years or for the rest of your life expectancy. They create a full life-care plan and assign a present value to all the expenses.

This work is often done in the litigation process but can also be done earlier if the case has significant-enough injuries and the policy limit is high enough to warrant it.

Property Damage

Some law firms help clients with this part of their case; however, this is one area where you don't necessarily need an attorney. The insurance company will give you an offer for property damage, and you can easily determine whether it's fair or you should ask for more. Just remember that the first offer is not necessarily the only or best offer. You can consult with a trusted body shop on the value of the damage to your vehicle. If your car is totaled, you can determine what it was worth by looking at Kelley Blue Book and used-car dealerships in your area that have similar vehicles with similar mileage. If you made recent repairs or did routine maintenance, that could increase the value of the vehicle as well (as long as you have receipts). Armed with this knowledge and documentation, you can talk with your adjuster to see if they are able to increase the value of the property-damage offer.

Personal Property Damage

Note that personal property damage is separate from the damage to your vehicle (i.e., property damage). Damage to personal property can include anything that was in your car during the accident, such as a laptop, child's car seat, or cellphone. Special damages should cover the cost of repairs or replacements.

This is an area where honesty and integrity are paramount. I've seen people lie about having more property damage than they actually did, which is an easy way to lose all credibility in your case if you get caught. If your iPhone screen was already cracked, don't say that it got broken in the accident. It's just not worth it.

Out-of-Pocket Expenses

These can include any other costs directly related to the accident, such as towing and storage fees for your vehicle, rental-car or ride-share expenses while your car is being repaired, and travel expenses for medical treatment. Again, keep track of all costs related to your accident that you think might qualify as special damages. Your attorney can help you sort it out from there. Keeping good records is crucial for maximizing the value of your claim.

In some cases, it's clear to the insurance company that a victim's special damages will easily exceed policy limits. As an example, I represented a client who was a longshore fisherman, and he relied on his hands to earn a living. He was in a motorcycle accident in which his hands and wrists suffered considerable damage requiring surgery, which affected his ability to return to work as a longshoreman. With these injuries, we were able to resolve his case fairly quickly at the maximum policy limit.

Bottom line is it's always better to work with a higher policy limit where the insurance company requires significant documentation to cover robust special damages. So if you're tasked with keeping incredibly good financial records for the foreseeable future, the good news is that you could have a large check on the horizon. Stay organized and be patient and your lawyer will work hard to maximize the value of your case.

CHAPTER 9

Paths to Resolution—Settling Your Case

After working with hundreds of clients, I can tell you with certainty that they all have the exact same question: "When will the case be over so I can move on with my life?" It's an excellent question because the legal process can feel like being in a prolonged state of limbo. You want to move forward and make progress, but for the most part, it just feels like a lot of waiting.

In Chapter 2, I shared a summary and timeline of the legal process. In this chapter, I expand on **Step 5: Settle your case and do a closing interview** so you know the different paths for resolving your case, as well as what you might be able to expect depending on what's happening with your unique situation.

A Brief Summary of the Legal Process

- Step 1: Do an intake and hire an attorney on a contingency fee
- Step 2: Seek proper medical treatment
- Step 3: Prepare demand
- Step 4: Negotiate
- Step 5: Settle your case and do a closing interview **(YOU ARE HERE)**
- Step 6: Conduct a closing interview

When you've focused on your recovery and documented all treatments, and a team of experts has helped clearly define the extent of your injuries, your attorney will consult with you on the potential total value of your case and get your approval to move forward. From there, they will put together a demand letter detailing the sum of money you're asking for to settle your case and send that letter to the insurance adjuster. This is the start of the negotiation process.

At this point, there are a wide variety of scenarios for how a case can play out. The first thing to know is that this process generally isn't quick. My clients usually picture this happening in a live meeting in which I share a number and the other side reacts in real time, but the demand letter is actually sent over email, and it typically takes more than a month for the adjuster to evaluate it.

Sometimes I hear back that the other side agrees to pay the full amount we asked for and the case will settle right away. The policy limits are low and my client's treatment easily surpasses the maximum, and the insurance company cuts a check quickly and a demand letter isn't even needed. I'll be honest: this is rare.

What's far more likely to happen is that the other side will counter with an amount that is significantly lower than the demand letter. From there, we go back and forth to determine whether we can reach a middle ground. During this process, I always keep my clients informed of the latest communication, providing my best advice for moving forward, although final decisions are always in their hands. For example, if the other side offers $50,000 and I think we can get $70,000, I will tell that to my client, but it's up to them whether to take the $50,000 and be done with it or keep pushing for a higher number.

Oftentimes, what my clients and I ask for and what the other side is willing to give are in two totally different stratospheres. But that doesn't mean we won't be able to find that middle ground and settle. In fact, a common negotiation strategy is to ask for an outrageously high number to start out, which the other side counters with an outrageously low amount. From there, going back and forth brings both sides closer to a reasonable number, and further conversations can help determine exactly what that looks like. Sometimes this same back-and-forth strategy is utilized, but with the opening numbers being closer to what you want your final number to be, with the belief that if your opening number is reasonable, you have a right to expect the insurer's opening number to be similarly reasonable. This could speed up negotiations as you won't be wasting time nickel-and-diming each other with offers and counteroffers that don't appreciably close the gap.

In some circumstances, generally when the policy limits might be low or modest, your attorney may demand a number that is truly the final offer, or very close to it, and make it clear to the insurer that there won't be any negotiating.

With any of these negotiating strategies, we are trying to determine whether it's possible to come to an agreement and settle. If the other side isn't offering what my client deserves, I recommend filing a lawsuit. By doing this, we are formally initiating the legal process and signaling to the defendant that we are willing to take the case to court. Not only is this the next necessary step in moving forward if negotiations break down, but it can also prompt the other party to take the claim more seriously, which is a major benefit.

If you have a significant injury case, the defense will take you more seriously, and if you have your doctors deposed, it will help with your lawsuit. If you have liability issues, it may make sense to file the lawsuit rather than accept 50-percent liability.

Note that once a lawsuit is filed, it's standard across the industry to pay a higher rate. Firms charge more because the case becomes more work. There will also be court fees that you need to pay directly, which is typically only a couple hundred dollars here and there. Considering the extra costs, your attorney will be able to advise on when filing a lawsuit will be worth it because they anticipate it will ultimately lead to a larger recovery. Remember that your attorney only gets paid if you get paid, so it's in their best interest to maximize your recovery.

Even when you move forward by filing a lawsuit, 90 percent of the time, your case will settle before you set foot in a courtroom. This happens for a variety of reasons:

Bandwidth/resources. Preparing for trial is a lot of work. We're talking months and months of preparation and potentially hundreds of hours put in by each law firm. On top of that, insurance attorneys work on many cases at the same time, so they are nothing if not busy. Depending on the insurance attorney's case load, your case might be a high-stakes assignment, or it could be small potatoes. Since they don't have unlimited resources, they need to choose where to best allocate their time and attention. When a case is relatively smaller compared with others, they aren't going to want to spend too much time dealing with it. After all, time is money.

In these situations, when I refuse to settle for a low offer and the other side sees how time-consuming it will be for them to go through all the steps to prepare for trial, they might be motivated to settle the case and pay more in order to protect their time.

This happened recently in a case where a deposition was scheduled, and since my client spoke English as a second language, they needed to hire an interpreter. The cost to do the deposition and pay the interpreter would all be paid by the insurance company, as is the standard. The deposition would take twice as long because everything would need to be translated back and forth. When opposing counsel thought about how much more time-intensive this would be, and how costs were already starting to add up on her side, she picked up the phone and said, "Give me a number." I gave her a number I thought she would never accept, but she did. My client got a lottery-winning result because we pressured the other side to put in work that didn't seem worth her time.

Personal obligations. When it comes to case timelines, attorneys don't always have much control. This is especially true for trial dates. Sometimes case schedules clash with personal commitments, such as weddings, graduations, or vacations. Other times, personal things come up and attorneys need to take time off to deal with them. In these situations, cases can settle quickly out of the blue.

One time I got a call from opposing counsel in one of my cases, and he told me he was busy with a personal thing that week: "I just don't have time to work on this case." He asked what number I needed in order to settle. Just like the last example, this put me in a place of power where I could ask for more than I otherwise would have, and I was able to settle the case for even more money than my client expected.

Chances at success in arbitration/trial. When you take a case all the way to arbitration or trial, you're putting the outcome in someone else's hands, whether it's a judge, an arbitrator, or a jury. To put everything on the line, you must be confident that you're going to get a favorable outcome. As a case develops and both sides go through the steps to prepare, information can come to light that makes you either more or less confident that a trial or arbitration will go in your favor.

For example, likability and honesty matter for both drivers involved in the crash. I once worked on a case in which the driver of the other car was rude and hostile during his deposition. He gave one-word answers and claimed over and over for hours to have no memory of how certain events had played out. There was no plausible reason or explanation for this mysterious memory loss, and it was clear that no one believed him. He came off like a real jerk—and a liar. To me, this was a positive development in the case because if a judge or jury would be turned off by him, they would be more likely to decide on a higher number for my client. The opposing counsel was well aware of this, and they called me soon after the deposition and offered more money to settle.

Uncomfortable with arbitration/trial. A surprisingly large number of attorneys don't like going to court and presenting in front of a judge or jury. Aside from the fact that it takes an incredible amount of time to prepare for court, it's a high-pressure situation that can be stressful. Even when attorneys are good at their job, many simply do not like this aspect of the work and thus try to avoid it. Attorneys who don't love going to court are always going to be more likely to settle as time goes by and the trial date looms over them. This can be a negotiation pressure point that I like to use against insurance defense attorneys. Personally, I love going to trial or arbitration because I relish being in the spotlight. If you are working with a different personal injury firm, make sure your attorney isn't a "trial/arbitration avoider."

I see settlement offers come in sporadically for my cases all the time. Sometimes it happens early on, and sometimes it takes longer. I generally see an influx of settlements in December because many insurance adjusters are eager to meet their yearly quota or performance goal. (They are often incentivized by the number of cases they close rather than the dollar amount for settlements.) Outside of that, good settlement offers often come out of the blue. But this only happens when we come from a place of strength. We do this by being prepared to go to trial or arbitration; otherwise, it looks like filing the lawsuit was just a bluff.

Your attorney will be able to advise you on the quality of the settlement offers that are coming in, and you should be aware of all of them so that you can make a choice on how to move forward. When you choose to accept an offer, you will be asked to sign a settlement agreement and release (a.k.a. a release agreement), which holds the other party harmless and dismisses the lawsuit. Once you sign the paperwork, it's final. You cannot go back on this choice later if you change your mind. (And when it's a good settlement offer, you won't want to!)

In the next chapter, we go into detail on how to go about what to expect in the litigation process.

CHAPTER 10

The Litigation Process

Once a lawsuit is filed, there is a specific process that both sides follow. The court identifies all the milestones and assigns deadlines so everyone knows what to expect. Below is a case schedule from King County, Washington, as an example. As you can see, from start to finish, the timeline is about one year.

Some of these milestones are technically optional, but to give you the best possible chance at maximizing your resolution, your attorney will participate in each of these steps. This not only makes your case as strong as possible, but it also shows that you are on top of everything and taking it seriously.

II. CASE SCHEDULE

*	CASE EVENT	EVENT DATE
	Case Filed and Schedule Issued.	03/21/2024
*	Last Day for Filing Statement of Arbitrability without a Showing of Good Cause for Late Filing [See KCLMAR 2.1(a) and Notices on Page 2]. **$250 arbitration fee must be paid**	08/29/2024
*	**DEADLINE** to file Confirmation of Joinder if not subject to Arbitration [See KCLCR 4.2(a) and Notices on Page 2].	08/29/2024
	DEADLINE for Hearing Motions to Change Case Assignment Area [KCLCR 82(e)].	09/12/2024

	DEADLINE for Disclosure of Possible Primary Witnesses [See *KCLCR 26(k)*].	10/21/2024
	DEADLINE for Disclosure of Possible Additional Witnesses [See *KCLCR 26(k)*].	12/02/2024
	DEADLINE for Jury Demand [see *KCLCR 38(b)(2)*].	12/16/2024
	DEADLINE for a Change in Trial Date [See *KCLCR 40(e)(2)*].	12/16/2024
	DEADLINE for Discovery Cutoff [See *KCLCR 37(g)*].	02/03/2025
	DEADLINE for Engaging in Alternative Dispute Resolution [See *KCLCR 16(b)*].	02/24/2025
	DEADLINE: Exchange Witness & Exhibit Lists & Documentary Exhibits [*KCLCR 4(i)*].	03/03/2025
*	**DEADLINE** to file Joint Confirmation of Trial Readiness [See *KCLCR 16(a)(1)*]	03/03/2025
	DEADLINE for Hearing Dispositive Pretrial Motions [See KCLCR 56; CR 56].	03/10/2025
*	Joint Statement of Evidence [See *KCLCR 4 (k)*].	03/17/2025
	DEADLINE for filing Trial Briefs, Proposed Findings of Fact and Conclusions of Law and Jury Instructions. (Do not file proposed Findings of Fact and Conclusions of Law with the Clerk.)	03/17/2025
	Trial Date [See *KCLCR 40*].	03/24/2025

The * indicates a document that must be filed with the Superior Court Clerk's Office by the date shown.

When a law firm chooses not to participate in all these steps, it sends a message that they are not prepared to go to trial. It's just like signing up for a marathon and failing to train. It's easy to see that you're falling behind, and it will be painful—if not impossible—to catch up later. It gets to a point where it's obvious you're wildly unprepared and that your shot at success is not great. This is important because, as we've discussed, cases can settle at any time—even after a lawsuit has been filed. And if you're unprepared for trial, it makes you look weak to the other side. Coming from a point of

If you're unprepared for trial, it makes you look weak to the other side.

weakness does not bode well for negotiations. The other side is likely to come in lower with any settlement offers, and they'll be less motivated to settle out of court because they think they have decent odds going up against you in a trial.

That's why my firm is highly organized and intentional about meeting every single milestone and fully participating in the litigation process. Yes, it's more work for us, but it's worth it because it gives us the best possible chance of maximizing the value of your case. If you're working with a different law firm, this is what you should expect from them too.

As the plaintiff in the case, you should anticipate being fully prepared as well. When you can hang in there and fully participate from start to finish, it will increase the value of your case. It also puts pressure on the other side—even if they are dealing with more intense deadlines or bigger cases. By being on top of your case and constantly pushing for the next steps to happen, you will get better outcomes than by just letting it simmer.

Your attorney will help you understand what is required from you, but the bottom line is that you need to follow instructions and meet your deadlines throughout all the steps in the litigation process.

Discovery

Litigation starts with the discovery process, which is just like it sounds: both sides are tasked with discovering all the details about the case so that they fully understand what happened in the accident and how you, the victim, have been impacted as a result. As the plaintiff, you play a crucial role in this process because you need to gather and share a great deal of information.

Most of my clients find this part both tedious and a bit intrusive. You won't know all the answers to the questions asked of you, and it will take time and energy for you to locate and verify all the relevant information. You'll also need to produce a wide range of documents, including financial and medical records and more. All this information will be carefully reviewed by the other side and used in the case.

Along those same lines, I always request all the information the defendant has so that I can gain a full understanding of the case and prepare for trial.

Discovery is broken down into three parts—interrogatories, admissions, and requests for production—and the deadlines for each part are typically 30 days.

Interrogatories. These are standard forms with a comprehensive list of open-ended questions. Here are some examples of the types of questions you can expect:

If you are currently or have previously been married, state for each marriage your spouse or former spouse's full name, date of birth, and maiden name (if any); present residence address; date and place of your marriage; and the date, place, and manner in which any previous marriage was terminated and the county and state in which the legal documents terminating the marriage were filed.

Did you, during the 24 hours prior to the INCIDENT, consume any alcoholic beverage, any drug, or any medication of any kind? If so, state the type or types of alcoholic beverage, drug, or medication, the amount of each, the time at which and the location where you took the alcoholic beverage, drug, or medication; and if you took a prescribed drug or medication, describe the condition for which it was taken and the name and address of the HEALTHCARE PROVIDER who prescribed it.

State your full name and any other names you have been known by during the last 10 years, your present address, date of birth, place of

birth, and Social Security number. In addition to your present ad-
dress, state all other addresses at which you have resided for the past
10 years and the dates you resided at each address.

All your answers need to be complete. For example, in the question that asks where you have lived in the past 10 years, you need to answer for all 10 years. If you only provide information for eight years because you can't remember all your prior addresses, it will only create more work for your law firm. They will comb through all your answers and point out the places where you need to go back and update your responses to make them complete. Is this a hassle for everyone? Yes. Do some of the answers seem completely unrelated to your accident? Absolutely. But this part of the process is not optional. By filing a lawsuit, the other side is entitled to all your answers in the interrogatories. So even if you feel frustrated or believe that answering detailed questions about your past is a waste of time or violation of your privacy, just remember that it's a required part of the process and that by completing these tasks, you are increasing the value of your claim.

Admissions. These are simple yes-or-no questions in which you admit or deny various things, such as having a valid driver's license and whether you have a restriction on your license. Admissions tend to be quicker to fill out than interrogatories, but getting the work done on time and truthfully is just as important.

Requests for production. Also known as RFPs, these are a variety of documents related to your case and are fair game for the other side to request. Whatever documents they ask for, you need to produce. For example, if you are making a wage-loss claim, they are entitled to your tax returns and pay stubs. And since your case is a personal injury case, they are entitled to your full medical records. (Your attorney will be able to assist in providing these, but you should know that the information can and will be shared with the other side at this point in the process.)

You probably won't have a lot of the requested documents, and if you do, they might not be lying around your house in a spot you can easily find. There's a good chance you'll need to dig for them or get someone else involved to obtain them, such as your tax preparer, your bookkeeper, the IRS, your doctor's office, or your employer's HR department. That's why it's so important to act quickly to review what is being asked for so that you can contact the appropriate people for help. It's likely that it could take them time to get back to you and send the documents you're looking for, and even then, the records could be incomplete and you might need to circle back for more information. If you put this process off until a week before it's due, you will put yourself and your case in a bad spot.

It's worth noting that all three of these steps in the discovery process are optional, but they should be done for every case. Good firms will complete all three steps for every case, but some firms skip them. I had a client come to me from another firm where his attorney had skipped these steps but had gotten him a $200,000 settlement offer that he was urged to take. My client thought the case was worth more, so he sought me out for a second opinion. I took the case and we did the hard work of completing all the optional steps to fully understand what a fair recovery could look like. This showed the other side how serious we were and what we could expect from going to trial. We ended up settling for seven figures.

Deposition

Your deposition is the first time when you have to participate in something related to the case in front of the other person's attorney. This step has a fancy name, but it's essentially just an interview. It's generally done in person in an office-like setting, but sometimes it's done over video instead. This process does not involve a judge, a jury, or any witnesses. It's just you, your attorney, the other side's attorney, and a court reporter who listens and transcribes every word that is said. If you speak English as a second language and need a translator, that person will be in attendance as well. Depositions usually only last a few hours, but they can go to a full day or longer in complex cases.

Most people get extremely nervous about their deposition. They're scared they will be yelled at by the other side's attorney and called a liar. I can assure you that this will not happen. I do not usually see defense attorneys getting aggressive with plaintiffs in depositions or asking sneaky questions to try to trick them. More often than not, defense attorneys are polite, professional, and very predictable when it comes to the questions they ask.

Although depositions are routine for attorneys, they feel like a big deal to clients. I want to be respectful of that and prepare my clients the best I possibly can so they feel comfortable and ready to do a great job. I always meet with clients directly before their deposition so they understand the primary goals and strategies. Small insights can go a long way in performance. Once clients are well versed in the process and know what to expect, we role-play the deposition so they can practice. Here are a few key things I focus on when training my clients:

Be likable and believable

When you are being deposed, your job is to show up and answer the questions asked of you by the other side's attorney. At this point, they have already read all the information you provided in the discovery phase. They've also gone through the medical records and probably know the case better than you do. In fact, they already know the answers to the vast majority of questions they will ask you. With this in mind, you might be wondering what the point is of having the deposition at all. The answer might surprise you. The most valuable information that insurance company attorneys are gleaning from the deposition process is related to *your personality*. They want to know what you would be like on the stand. Are you a believable witness? Are you likeable, or even better (or worse, from their perspective)—lovable? Or do you get angry easily and lose your cool? Do you come across as obstinate, combative, or rude? All these things matter.

When you take a case to arbitration or trial, you're putting the resolution into someone else's hands. Facts guide the case, but there's an indelible human element as well. People generally don't like to support jerks or liars, and these kinds of individuals don't do as favorably in court as do kind, lovable people who pull at your heartstrings. In a deposition, the defense attorney is trying to gauge where you fall on the likability and believability spectrum. They will record their observations about your demeanor and personality and include it in the report they share with the insurance company after the deposition. This information helps guide next steps in terms of a settlement offer. That's why it's so important to stay levelheaded and focus on coming across as likable and sincere.

Anticipate the right questions

Your attorney should give you a solid rundown of the types of questions you can anticipate and help you practice answering. For example, it's pretty much a guarantee that you will be asked to describe in your own words how the accident occurred. In addition to this, every case has questions around liability and injury. You will probably be asked why you got certain types of medical treatment and where you went for treatment. When you know what questions to expect, you can practice the answers ahead of time and reduce your anxiety.

Depending on your case, you might want to prepare for answering questions that feel extremely personal. For example, if part of your claim relates to loss of intimacy, you should expect to be asked questions about how frequently you had sex before the accident and how often you are having sex now. These are legitimate legal questions that are not meant to embarrass you, pick on you, or discredit your story. The answers are needed to help assess damages and establish a fair value for your case. Highly personal questions can be emotional, so it's in your best interest to work with your attorney before the deposition so that you have a clear idea of what you can expect and don't feel blindsided.

Keep in mind that depositions are not made public and that answering tough questions helps get you one step closer to maximizing your case value.

Don't overshare

When you're being questioned by an attorney, less is more. You just want to answer the exact question that is being asked, rather than expanding on the answer as you would if you were chatting with a friend. Here's an example:

Do you know what time it is?

The correct answer to that question is not the current time. It's either yes or no. Do not give more than you are being asked to give. That's how you accidentally say something that you can't take back and damage the value of your case.

When you finish answering a question, if the attorney keeps looking at you like they expect you to continue, bite your tongue. They don't necessarily think you *should* say more—they're just hoping you will go off on a tangent and share information that could weaken your case. Don't fall for this tactic.

Take it slowly

There's no need to rush your answers in a deposition. In fact, the best way to do a good job and prevent yourself from oversharing is by taking your time. After a question is asked, you want to pause so you can think carefully before you provide a thoughtful, succinct response. If it feels strange to slow down the pace of the question-answer exchange, it can help to keep in mind that the court reporter is listening and transcribing every word. It's actually beneficial to them that people don't talk over one another by answering too quickly.

Another smart reason to pause is because it gives your attorney time to object to a question. There are certain things that, for various reasons, you aren't required to answer, and you aren't going to know what they are unless your attorney interjects. Allow time for this to happen. If you hear your attorney say "objection," stop speaking immediately—even if you're mid-sentence.

You don't have to know everything

You might be asked how many times you went for certain types of treatments, and on what dates. Remember: this information has already been shared in the discovery packet, so the other side has access to it and the attorney probably has it right in front of them when they ask the questions. No one is expecting you to commit all the details of your case to memory. That's not why you're being questioned. What's really being tested is the way in which you respond. Will you become annoyed or frustrated by questions you can't answer? Will you make wild guesses that seem like lies instead of admitting that you don't know an answer? Will you get nervous and shut down? Or will you stay calm, cool, and collected when you're put on the spot? Remember that likability is paramount and having a memory like a steel trap is not required.

Mediation

After each party's deposition, mediation is a required step in the litigation process. That's because the court system does not have the bandwidth to accommodate all the lawsuits that are filed. Court schedules get backed up by many months and it's preferred for parties to settle out of court, if at all possible. Parties are required to make "a good-faith effort" in mediation as an alternative dispute resolution before going to court. This means both sides must schedule a meeting, attend, and at least have a short conversation.

Mediation is facilitated by a mediator who is a neutral party chosen and agreed upon by the attorneys. The goal of the mediator is to get an agreement from the parties so that the case can be resolved. There are some great mediators out there. Many are retired judges who have a strong understanding of where both parties are coming from and what a fair resolution looks like.

Mediation is typically scheduled for a half-day session, and it's often done online, where each side is given a breakout room to have private conversations. Just like in a deposition, it's important to come across as likable to the mediator. They are supposed to be impartial, but they will work harder for you if they like you. They also recognize that if they like you, a judge or jury will probably like you, and that makes your case stronger.

If the mediation session doesn't end in a resolution but the parties have come closer to reaching an agreement, the mediator will recommend scheduling another session to continue negotiations. This will go on until the case settles or it becomes clear that the case will not settle without going to arbitration or trial.

Arbitration

If your case is valued at less than $100,000, you have the option to do arbitration as an alternative to going to trial. Instead of going to court and having a judge or jury decide on the resolution, an arbitrator is given this power. Just like in mediation, the arbitrator is a neutral party, and both sides have some say in selecting the individual.

Arbitration is a simplified way to resolve cases that are on the smaller end compared with what comes through the court system. In this process, both sides make their argument, and witness testimony is included in written documents rather than having the witnesses appear in person. From there, an arbitrator reviews all the information, and they circle back a few days later via email with a ruling.

It's important to note that by turning down settlement offers and going to arbitration or trial, you are turning down guaranteed money and taking a chance at the unknown. It's possible that you could be awarded less than you were offered as a settlement. It's also possible that you will lose and get nothing. I will say that this is very rare and only happens in situations where a defendant isn't found to be liable. Your attorney should always discuss the possibility of this happening so that you can weigh the risks and benefits of continuing to move forward with arbitration or trial.

Trial

This is what you see on TV and what you probably think of when you consider being involved in a lawsuit. When it comes to personal injury cases, going to trial is rare. Even when it seems like your case is headed to trial, it will probably settle sometime in the year before your court date. But as I've said throughout this book, it's important to move forward as though you are going to trial. Part of this is understanding what it will be like so that you can mentally prepare.

Personal injury trials can range from a couple days to about a month depending on the number of witnesses and complexity. There is a judge, attorneys on both sides, and usually a jury. There's also a court clerk and judicial assistant. Sometimes, members of the public can be in the room to watch the trial. Witnesses are called to the stand, and both attorneys can ask them questions. You and the defendant will also take turns on the witness stand, with both parties' attorneys asking you questions.

Your attorney should prep you for answering questions, much like before the deposition. All the same key points for doing well in depositions should be applied to taking the stand in a trial. But at this point in the process, even more time and effort should go into preparing you since the pressure will be dialed up a bit higher during cross-examination. You need to make sure that you have a good understanding of what is likely to be asked of you and then practice your answers. You should do this in a role-playing scenario in which the other person gets tough with you, like the defense attorney will do in court. Going through that in a practice round makes a difference later because you already know what it feels like to be in that scenario. It isn't necessarily pleasant, but it's less shocking if you've already fielded tough questions from your own attorney.

Aside from how you speak on the witness stand, your appearance matters. You need to show up to court on time and dress appropriately. Don't fidget or chew gum. Pay attention and look at whomever is speaking. Be conscious of your facial expressions. Bring a notepad and pen so you can jot down questions you might have or notes for your attorney so they can also pay attention to the testimony. Above all else, tell the truth and do your best to come across as likable and sincere.

At the end of the trial, the judge or jury will take time to deliberate before everyone eventually gets called back in to hear the verdict. No matter what that verdict is, remember that you're in a courtroom and expected to conduct yourself appropriately.

In the end, you and your attorney should do the best you possibly can throughout the litigation process in order to drive the best possible outcome. Going through all the steps to prepare for trial can feel like a pain, but it's only temporary. And the stress of being cross-examined can feel overwhelming at times, but ultimately, it's worth it. If you can push through the discomfort, there should be a reward on the other side.

CHAPTER 11

Getting Paid and Moving On

This is arguably the most satisfying part of the process! The long and difficult journey has finally come to an end. After all the time and effort, it's a great feeling to wrap it all up and help people move forward with their lives.

This is the point you'll get to after you reach a resolution in your case. There are a few things you should know about the final step in your journey.

To start, it can take a bit of time to get paid. If you reach a resolution in arbitration or trial, the insurance company has a right to appeal within 20 days. Though this is unlikely, an appeal would hold up the resolution of your case significantly. During this time period, you could be in a holding pattern, waiting to see what will happen. If they appeal the verdict, it's essentially taking a step back and officially revisiting the case. This would mean going through arbitration or trial a second time, which could result in a very different outcome. Although this does not often happen, it's possible.

Once the resolution is finalized, the money can officially move in your direction from the insurance company. Many entities may need to be paid, including your lawyer and numerous medical providers. The standard way this is handled is for the insurance company to pay your attorney, who then takes the lead paying the proper amounts to everyone you owe. They also deduct their attorney fee from your resolution. This is documented through a settlement memorandum, which includes an itemized list of fees. Even if the insurance company pays right away, it usually takes two to six weeks for law firms to finalize this list. Some firms take much longer. They could have your payment sitting in their account for months before they can do the work to figure out how it should be divvied up to pay the entities that are owed.

After these calculations are complete, sometimes the final number isn't as high as you would want it to be due to expenses. For example, if your attorney is making more money than you, you should ask why. This doesn't happen at my firm, but I've seen it happen at many others. Medical expenses are often a big part of this issue. Your law firm can work with your healthcare providers to ensure that you haven't been overcharged for services, which can happen from time to time, with patients not realizing that they've been overbilled. Additionally, a good law firm can help negotiate with healthcare providers to see if they would be willing to accept less money than whatever was billed, especially if the patient is ending up taking home a small amount of money after a settlement. (Attorneys don't get paid extra for this, but a good firm will do it to help you.)

Money and the Government

The government isn't usually involved when you get your check. You don't have to pay taxes on the money, which is great news! However, when you have this money coming in, you should be aware that it can affect other money or benefits that you have coming in from the government, such as unemployment, Social Security, and/or retirement benefits. If you think this might apply to you, speak with your attorney during your case so you know what to expect.

Related to this, if you owe the government money, your check can be docked as a way for it to collect what it's owed. For example, if you have a child-support lien, it must be paid before you can collect any of the money from your case.

And if you are a minor, the court usually requires that your settlement money be deposited into a special bank account that your parents or guardians cannot access. The money stays blocked in this account until you turn 18 and can withdraw from it directly.

For other financial and tax implications regarding your recovery check, contact a good financial advisor.

New Money

Did you know that nearly a third of lottery winners go bankrupt within three to five years?[9] When you're used to being a working-class person and you suddenly have tens of thousands of dollars, or even hundreds of thousands of dollars, it puts you in an interesting position. It's a life-changing amount of money. With your bank account padded, it can feel like the world is your oyster. You are able to get out of debt, buy your dream house, travel the world, take care of your extended family, and fund a retirement account. And of course, there's also designer clothes, shoes, drugs, alcohol, gambling, and who knows what else. Some of the ways you spend your money can last for decades or even generations. Or you can blow through it all in a couple months.

When you're not used to having large sums of money, the best thing you can do for yourself is to work with a trusted financial advisor to help you properly allocate your liquidity in a way that aligns with your goals. (Please note that I am not a financial advisor and this is not financial advice.) But just about everyone can agree that being strategic about money will make a major difference years down the line.

For example, if you've always been a renter, buying your first home can be a smart financial move—especially if you can pay cash instead of dealing with a mortgage.

Paying off expensive debt can be another priority. Credit-card interest is often at the top of the list of things you don't want to pay if you don't have to.

You might also want to look into risk-conscious investing. A large chunk of money invested properly will make money just sitting there. For example, if you have $500,000 in a high-yield savings account and the bank gives you 5 percent interest on that money, you make $25,000 a year—for doing nothing! You don't even have to risk your money in the stock market. This is one way the rich get richer.

And if you're years away from retirement, investing in the market is also a great option for growing your money over time. Yes, there are risks associated with stocks, but overall, history has shown us that people who invest their money in an index fund over many decades have ended up making a lot of money, thanks in large part to the compound interest.

Certain financial choices can also make a significant difference in how much you owe in taxes at the end of the year. I recommend talking to an expert about this so you make the right decisions.

Coming into a large sum of money all at once is a crucial time in your life, and you need to be honest with yourself about your ability to handle it in a responsible way. If you have a tendency to spend money carelessly or you're struggling with addiction, it's

Coming into a large sum of money all at once is a crucial time in your life, and you need to be honest with yourself about your ability to handle it in a responsible way.

especially important to put extra effort into getting help and safeguarding against blowing your settlement money.

One of my clients recognized that she struggled with drug addiction and told me she was worried about what she would do after collecting her check. Even though I was ready to pay her, she told me she wasn't in a place in her life where she felt like she was in a good mental condition to take the money. She wanted to spend more time in rehab and get into a better place where she felt like she had more control over her impulses. She chose to take time to herself and put in the work. About four months after she could have picked up the check, she finally let me know that she was ready to stop by. My team and I were so proud of her! She showed an incredible amount of self-awareness and restraint by holding off on picking up her check until she was in a place where she could make the best possible decisions for herself in the long term. We are still in touch with her, and we've been thrilled to see that she's been responsible with her money and is living a healthy new life.

Another element to consider when coming into a lot of cash is how family members and friends might behave. Chances are that everyone knows what you've had on the line for a long time. Sometimes my clients see people coming out of the woodwork to ask them for money. Maybe a friend just needs $500 to keep their lights on this month—and then $200 for groceries next month. Or their extended family wants to go on vacation with them and they expect all the expenses to be covered. Spending a little on family and friends here and there is a generous thing to do, and it feels good to be in a position to help people and make them happy. But doing so quickly adds up. If you aren't careful, you can blow through a massive amount of cash before you know it.

A great strategy for preventing this is by working with a financial advisor to help you invest money into the kinds of accounts where you can't withdraw it at any time without a penalty. For example, with a Roth IRA, the money grows tax-free until you're 65 years old. You can withdraw it before then, but you'll take a big financial hit. When you have these kinds of accounts, it helps you get into the mentality that the money isn't just sitting around for you to spend at any time. You can also proactively let friends and family know that your financial advisor has stashed your funds into various accounts for retirement and you don't even have easy access to that money. That way, if they ask to "borrow" a little cash, they know it isn't as simple for you as just going to the ATM. If you say you need to get a financial advisor involved to withdraw the money, it can be a great way to deflect attempts to deplete your savings.

It's also smart to make sure friends and family know that you aren't taking home the total amount that was awarded to you in your recovery. Once you pay your medical bills and your attorney's fees, you're likely to be left with less than half of the total. As an example, a $1,000,000 settlement can turn into a $400,000 check for you. That makes a major difference in what you actually have versus what people think you have.

On top of this, you might need to remind friends and family that you need to keep some of your recovery money for future expenses resulting from your accident. Rehabilitation isn't cheap, and if your earning ability has been compromised as a result of your injury, you need to be especially conservative with your finances.

Walking away with a significant settlement check is an excellent way to resolve your case. You'll see why it was worth the extra time and effort to be patient and do your best to reach MMI. When the money is deposited in your bank account, make it count! You went through a lot to get here, and you owe it to yourself to be smart about how you spend it.

Moving Forward: Safety First

After being injured in a car accident and going through a personal injury lawsuit, you probably don't ever want to go through it again.

Most of my clients are one-time clients, but my firm does have a handful of folks who have been injured in multiple car accidents that were not their fault. We hate seeing people go through this kind of trauma once, but a second, third, or even fourth time is excruciating.

Accidents often happen out of nowhere and there's nothing you can do in the moment to prevent them. But there are a lot ways to decrease your risks. Here are some important statistics around when car accidents tend to occur:

- There are more fatal auto accidents in the summer and early fall months (June through October) because there are more cars out on the road. Think family vacations, road trips, dropping kids off at college, etc. During the winter months, both vehicle miles and deaths go down.[10]

- On average in 2022, fatal car crashes were more frequent on weekends, peaking on Saturdays. The number of non-fatal crashes tended to be higher on weekdays, peaking on Fridays.[11]
- For both fatal and nonfatal crashes, the peak time of day was 4 p.m. to 7:59 p.m.[12]
- Alcohol-impaired driving crashes are significantly higher in the evening and early morning hours.[13]
- Holidays and weekends typically have significantly more accidents than do other days. This includes Memorial Day, Independence Day, Labor Day, Thanksgiving, Christmas, and New Year's Eve.[14]
- On average, there are more than 5.8 million vehicle crashes each year. Approximately 21 percent of these crashes— over 1.2 million—are weather related. Weather-related crashes are defined as those that occur in adverse weather (e.g., rain, sleet, snow, fog, severe crosswinds, blowing snow/sand/debris) or on slick pavement (e.g., wet pavement, snowy/slushy pavement, icy pavement). On average, nearly 5,000 people are killed and over 418,000 people are injured in weather-related crashes each year.[15]
- The vast majority of weather-related crashes happen on wet pavement and during rainfall: 70 percent on wet pavement and 46 percent during rainfall. A much smaller percentage of such crashes occur during winter conditions: 18 percent during snow or sleet, 13 percent on icy pavement, and 16 percent snowy or slushy pavement. Only 3 percent happen in the presence of fog.[16]

With all this in mind, it's smart to reduce your time on the road and consider avoiding driving conditions that present a higher risk of accidents. To start, a long work commute exposes you to significantly more risk over time than does working from home, walking to work, or taking public transit. (Living closer to work is better for your stress level too!)

In terms of timing, if you need to run errands that can be done in the morning or early afternoon, that's a better option for avoiding peak accident hours and drunk drivers. Also, pay attention to the weather. If the roads are wet or icy, there's a greater risk of accident. If you don't need to drive in those conditions, don't.

And when it comes to traveling, if you're considering taking a long road trip, check out flights instead. During holiday weekends, if you can fly somewhere or stay local and keep off the roads, those are great options.

Aside from choosing when and where to drive, make sure you and your passengers always wear your seatbelts and that your car has all the safety features working, particularly the airbags. Don't drive after you've been drinking or when you're overly tired. Refrain from texting while driving or doing anything else that takes your eyes off the road.

Check Your Insurance Coverage

This is your final reminder to review your auto-insurance coverage and make sure you have what you need. Do you have PIP? Do you have UIM protection? If not, it's highly recommended that you get it ASAP. Also check to see if you can afford to increase your policy limits.

Being injured in a car accident is scary, but know that you are not alone. When you hire an attorney and their law firm who have the right knowledge, they will make the journey as easy as possible for you. Keep following the advice in this book and have faith that there is light at the end of the tunnel.

Acknowledgments

To the indomitable team at our law firm, whose resilience, dedication, and unwavering commitment to our clients redefine what it means to be champions of the law. Each day, you demonstrate the profound impact of collective effort, integrity, and compassion. This journey, with its highs and lows, has been enriched by your loyalty, expertise, and relentless pursuit of what is right. You are not just colleagues but also the very backbone of our success and the architects of our future.

To the Pithy Wordsmithery team and my writing coach, Amelia Forczak. I would not have had the ability to finish this project without your leadership, steady hand on my shoulder pushing me forward, and grace with my difficult schedule. I would still be metaphorically trapped in a Portland blizzard were it not for you!

And to my mom, the quintessential pillar of strength and encouragement. Your boundless support, even in moments when it seemed embarrassing, has been my unwavering source of courage and inspiration. Your belief in me, often stronger than my own, has propelled me through challenges and guided me toward achievements I once thought unattainable. This dedication is but a small token of my immense gratitude for your unconditional love and the sacrifices you've made. You've taught me that, with tenacity and love, anything is possible.

This book is a tribute to all of you whose support and influence have left an indelible mark on both my personal and professional life. Together, we continue to strive toward making a difference, one case, one client, one community at a time.

About the Author

Joshua Brumley has a passion for educating all communities as a car-crash law resource. He is a Washington state native, raised in the Tacoma area. After graduating from the University of Washington, he earned his MBA at Jacksonville University and completed his law degree at Florida Coastal School of Law. Joshua has practiced as an attorney with the Washington State  Bar Association since 2015. He has served as a pro tem judge and is the owner of Brumley Law Firm, whose mission is to empower our community by providing client-focused service, one car crash at a time.

Community involvement in the South Sound region is important to Joshua. In addition to serving on the board of directors for the Pierce County Center for Dispute Resolution, he is a member of the Puyallup Tribal Bar, Tulalip Tribal Bar, South King County Bar Association, and Federal Bar Association and has served two terms as president of the YL Division of the Tacoma-Pierce County Bar Association. He has served as a barrister member of American Inns of Court and is dedicated to promoting the highest levels of professionalism in the practice of law.

As the managing attorney at Brumley Law Firm, Joshua works daily to ensure that his team delivers the most professional and supportive legal services in Western Washington. This dedication is among the many reasons his peers recognized him in the select group of Rising Stars of the 2020, 2021, 2022, and 2023 Super Lawyers survey, and in 2024, he and his firm earned the title "Law Firm of the Year" at the 2024 Sharkey Awards.

References

1. "American Driving Survey," Andrew Gross, September 13, 2023.
2. "How Many Car Accidents Occur Each Hour, Day & Year in the U.S.?" Amaro Law Firm, March 29, 2023, https://amarolawfirm.com/how-many-car-accidents-occur-each-hour-day-year-in-the-u-s/#:~:text=Car%20accidents%20are%20a%20leading,19%2C937%20crashes%20every%20day.
3. "Personal Injury Statistics: The Difference a Lawyer Can Make," Villarreal & Begum, May 23, 2023, https://www.vblawgroup.com/blog/firm-news/personal-injury-statistics-the-difference-a-lawyer-can-make/.
4. "What Is the Average Cost of a Car Accident?" The Intelligent Driver, August 26, 2020, https://www.theintelligentdriver.com/2020/08/26/what-is-the-average-cost-of-a-car-accident/.
5. "Personal Injury Statistics: The Difference a Lawyer Can Make," Villarreal & Begum.
6. "The Average Cost of Medical & Hospital Bills After A Car Accident," accessed July 12, 2024, https://lawyers.law.com/legal/medical-visits/average-cost.html.
7. Spinal stenosis, Mayo Clinic website, https://www.mayoclinic.org/diseases-conditions/spinal-stenosis/symptoms-causes/syc-20352961#:~:text=Spinal%20stenosis%20happens%20when%20the,spinal%20stenosis%20have%20no%20symptoms.
8. Shankuan Zhu et al., "BMI and Risk of Serious Upper Body Injury Following Motor Vehicle Crashes: Concordance of Real-World and Computer-Simulated Observations," National Library of Medicine, March 30, 2010, https://www.ncbi.nlm.nih.gov/pmc/articles/PMC2846859/.

9. Eric Lagatta, "Lotto regret: Pitfalls of Powerball, lottery winners serve as cautionary tales as jackpots swell," *USA Today*, July 19, 2023, https://www.usatoday.com/story/news/nation/2023/07/19/powerball-mega-millions-winners-instant-billionaire-regrets/70430571007/#:~:text=Nearly%20 one%2Dthird%20of%20lottery,Financial%20Planner%20 Board%20of%20Standards.

10. "Crashes by month," NSC Injury Facts, accessed May 9, 2024, https://injuryfacts.nsc.org/motor-vehicle/overview/ crashes-by-month/.

11. "Crashes by time of day and day of week," NSC Injury Facts, accessed May 9, 2024, https://injuryfacts.nsc.org/motor-vehicle/ overview/crashes-by-time-of-day-and-day-of-week/.

12. Ibid.

13. Christy Bieber, "Car accident statistics 2023," *Forbes*, January 23, 2023, https://www.forbes.com/advisor/legal/car-accident-statistics/.

14. "Holiday Traffic Fatality Estimate," NSC Injury Facts, accessed May 7, 2024, https://injuryfacts.nsc.org/motor-vehicle/holidays/ holiday-introduction/.

15. Ten-year averages from 2007 to 2016 analyzed by Booz Allen Hamilton, based on NHTSA data; "How do weather events impact roads?" US Department of Transportation, Road Weather Management Program, accessed May 9, 2024, https://ops.fhwa.dot. gov/weather/q1_roadimpact.htm.

16. Ibid.

Made in the USA
Las Vegas, NV
26 September 2024

95825090R00080